THINGS OF THAT NATURE

THINGS *of* THAT NATURE

words for the mystic heart

DR. BETHANNE K.W.

2019
GOLDEN DRAGONFLY PRESS

FIRST PRINT EDITION, November 2019
FIRST EBOOK EDITION, November 2019

ISBN–13: 978–1–7330099–0–4
ISBN–10: 1–7330099–0–6

Library of Congress Control Number: 2019948713

Printed on acid-free paper supplied by a
Forest Stewardship Council-certified provider.

First published in the United States of America
by Golden Dragonfly Press, 2019.

www.goldendragonflypress.com

for the seekers, the dreamers, the magic makers, and anyone who has ever listened to their heart and followed its bliss: I believe in you.

let's uphold each other in the light and keep reaching up- high and sky-wide, emboldening each other to shine bright.

LIFE INTENTIONS

I want to be happy and creative.

I want to learn from nature and have her teach me her medicine and mysteries.

I want to see and know how beautiful and magical and divine I am— exactly as I am right now.

I want to see the magic in the every day.

I want to cultivate joy

I want to write poetry about crystals and the moon and love and things of that nature.

I want to embrace change, all while still appreciating the gifts of right now.

I want to keep my heart open and never forget everything has its own wisdom to offer.

I want to make each day count and find value in the smallest things.

I want to empower myself (and others) to love where we are planted.

Unicorn, rainbow, and fairy believer.

GREETINGS & SALUTATIONS

About a year and a half ago, on a rainy afternoon where the jungle felt extra inky and my thoughts felt extra thinky, I had an unexpected epiphany.

At the time, I was in a transitory space in my life where I was feeling like a malcontent calico cat, who wasn't satisfied either inside or outside and kept pacing back and forth between settings, trying to find something that settled and suited.

I'd been living in Kauai for about 9 months after a soul calling led me to leave my well-rooted life in Alaska, transplant to the island, and see what spirit had waiting for me here. As grateful as I was to be on Kauai, I have to admit I often wished my life was somewhere other than where it was that first year.

I wanted to be more well-formed, more certain of my future work, with a wider reach and bigger name than what I was. I wanted to be the me I hope I'll be in about 3 to 4 years-time. Instead, I was spring of 2018 me. A newbie on the island who was often confused, raw, reforming and reassembling my pieces.

I wanted to be ahead of myself, be someone and somewhere that I wasn't. Instead, I was who I was, how I was, exactly where I was at.

It was one of those flashes of clarity that comes over a second cup of coffee, with misty jungle scenes and a warm dog lolling on one's lap: *Joy is happening right now, and you're missing it.*

I was missing it. The more I focused on where I wasn't, the more I was missing out on where I was. My deeper self was speaking, and I was listening. Losing my brother in 2016 had taught me a lot about cherishing the gift of life and my moments of being, and I realized I was out of alignment with my lessons.

So, I got out my neon glitter pens and whipped out a life intention list filled with all sorts of whimsical, mystical, lyrical desires that suited my intuitive, magical soul. Somewhere on that list was an intention to "write poetry about crystals, the moon, and love, and *things of that nature.*"

About six months later, still in a space of career rebuilding and restructuring my life, I was thinking about "what would my heart wish to create if I cared less about the results and just about the joy of creation?"

"I would publish another poetry book!" immediately came to mind. And it just so happened, that because I had followed my heart's edicts to write moon-touched, crystal-inspired, love-swept poetry—I had a whole bunch of poems sitting on my computer, asking to be gathered into a bigger collection.

This book is a result of those poems.

Poetry offers the writer and reader a gift—the ability to zoom in on a moment and feel into it. *Dream into it. Imagine into it. Channel into it.* Receive, see and listen with our soul's eyes and heart's wise and drop into worlds we often miss when we're not truly hearing or seeing.

Poetry is a bridge into other realms. The imagination becomes a vehicle that travels us there. Words become the galactic center of mystic journeying, and there is much truth to be found in that space.

I still have my "Life Intentions" list hanging on my wall. I'm still forming in my new Kauai life, so I refer to it whenever I feel I'm losing my way and forgetting to *Joy* and *Be*. The list is a heart-compass that brings me back to my true north.

Sometimes in those moments where I'm connected to my heart's needle, I'll grab my laptop and pull up a blank page. Stare at the moon outside, flip out the odd tarot card, or get lost in the music coming from the rain. On days where my poet's muse is riding high, inspired words will slip-stream out onto the screen. Sky-rhymes, half-notes, and dream-stories of forgotten places and things.

We'll dance together, the words and I, and I remember that the best magic is found in the every day for those who have the heart-eyes to see.

Aloha and Mahalo,

Dr. Beth Anne KW

TABLE OF CONTENTS

☞ *Colors, Candles & Crystals*

☞ *Emotions, Oceans & Potions*

☞ *Trees, Transitions & Transfigurations*

Magic, Muse & Mystery

life's A
beAch &
You'RE A
peAch!

8

8

Colors, Candles

&

Crystals

things of nature, hearth, flowers and fairies

When the first baby laughed for
the first time, its laugh broke into
a thousand pieces, and they

all went skipping about, and that
was the beginning of fairies.

J.M. Barrie, Peter Pan

fly

CRYSTAL CRESCENDO

Blue kyanite, peach aventurine
rainbow moonstones
send me sings.

Songs of soft
where kind is the dream,
a percussion of peace
rings on rose tambourines.

Where hibiscus strums
with rubellite keys
and sea's crystal heart
drums and thrums in like beat.

Hush and drop deep
(can you hear the earth speak?)
let's stop and still for a while—
and listen to her music.

WHEN IN NATURE

I think it's all going
to be okay
when I'm in nature,
the rain washes
anything bad away

the worries
I carry
are reduced:
to drops
& trickles
of midnight dew

when I'm in nature
I find love's still
in the beat of earth's heart,
there is a precision
of fluid start—

and end,
and in-between
of day's
cycle,
and set,
and golden mean

things feel
kinder and gentler;
more reassured outdoors,

clouds shake awake
and change shape:
gateways to imagination's
shores

where things
don't matter
so much
except for angel's soft song
and water's calm pour . . .

and flow
and ebb,
and the way
the old falls away
into sky's misty gray,
to be transformed
into dawn
of new day

life is transient
in this space;
I find my place;
breathe in grace;
feel love's pace
(remember that courage
always finds a way)

and when I'm in nature
I know everything's
going to be
okay.

FLOWER TALK

There are so many truths
you can learn from
a flower:

When to keep open
and when to gently close.

How to blow in the direction
of the ever-changing
breeze.

How to learn to grow,
then bloom, in the space life
plants us.

I talk to the petals
in tender exchange,
tell them of my stream of life,
and listen to their bright light
on the stem,
as I bring myself back
to the truth of the buds—

Love is the only thing
that can teach us
how to let ourselves become
full again.

ORCHID BLUES

Find the spaces love is growing and plant your seeds there. Learn how to embody a bigger self by refusing to capitulate to judgment or fear.

Make quantum leaps in your heart that take you from a space of shame to grace. Follow your soul rhythms and let them play you a different kind of music; teach yourself to move to them and become the sea. Whisper with palm fronds and listen to stones, invite the fairies to come in and sing. *Hum wind songs with wild abandon and tap dance to rain's drops and pings.*

Tune in as the orchids strum the blues: there is healing through grief and more courage for truth. Create a gentle uproar with your gracious refusal to be anybody but you.

CHASING FAIRIES

She is the first mountain
I ever climbed.

8-years-old,
I think I can,
one foot in front of the other,
because I didn't want to quit
and thought I heard
the songs of fairies
hidden in her gardens
and went in chase.

Today,
magenta mixed with
mahogany erase—
muddy treks
and white flecks
and tundra collects
and hides 10,000 Who's
in its specks—
I almost hear their
joyous noise
over the thunks of my
earth-slick steps.

This mountain,
she hides
all her mysteries
in her wrinkles
and her lines.
Blink—
and you will miss them,
her portals to the divine.

Things unseen,
yet still alive,
worlds within worlds
on her face reside,
and just as I did
way back when,
I go in chase of
the invisible,
mystical,
unfathomable,
foreseeable—
(if you have the eyes)

Her magic waits in
the in-betweens,
earth's kaleidoscope
of rhymes.

HER SOUL WAS AN OPEN WINDOW

the pristine
pink
of a peony
teaches her
to unfold
when it's time;

a blade of
grass,
a verdant stripe
among many,
about humility
and belonging
to the whole;

a lazy cat
watches clouds drift
as dandelions sift
and seasons shift;
and summer's swift
sweet gifts
etch imprints
of hope

against the window
of her soul

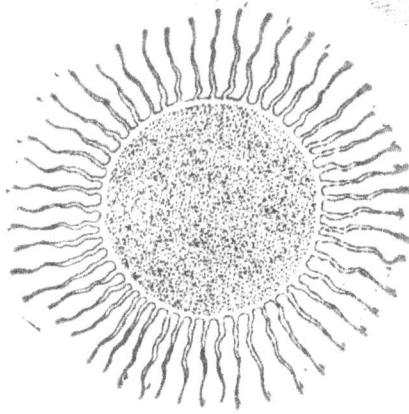

TREE & EMPATHY

Let yourself unwind
on day's new breeze.
Look for the good
and notice the ease.
Find the magic when you
feel your lungs breathe—

Tea, trees, empathy
(then repeat).

Home

They echo off
of each other
1 rooster.
2 rooster.
3 rooster.
Crow!

Clucking
and doodling
amidst the
waving green
where
avocados ripe,
and oranges pipe,
and papayas hide
on treetop's high.

The winds
sweep eternal,
the clouds
shifting shades,
and the rain
comes in waves
to the sound
of sky's veins.

They say home
is where the
heart is,
*(though my heart
is much too free
to be defined by
just one place).*

But my
starseed soles
and wandering loll
and mermaid's toll
*(who rings with
the bells of sea
breeze soul)*
tell me my feet
have a place to
come home;

*I can be unrestrained
in the heart of this space*

Duet of Possibility

F ind grace for your process today. Be in duet with the calm of the trees.

Inhale then exhale and mindfully send a troubling situation in your life *breath*. Invite greater grace in for all involved. Look up at the sky as you breathe.

Remember you are so much more than your mental chatter and history. *Embrace the grace-space of your own possibility.*

Tapestries

Let it unspool
at its own pace…
in small threads,
giant unravelings,
weavings and
reweavings
of tapestry
and soul.

Trusting life's
fabric to knit
itself full—
with soft blush silks
and rough red bolts:
a patchwork
of moments,
which collage
our taproot
of whole.

Sea greens,
opal creams,
russet dreams,
peach scenes,
emerald beams,
and onyx coals—

We reform,
reknit,
release,
renew
every breath
and beat
we sow.

Things the Flower Says

Be so gentle
that they never see you coming,
and when the moment is ripe—
surprise them all
with your presence,
and *Bloom*.

COLOR THERAPY

Sometimes colors are needed instead of words: Gentle mahoganies and rubellite trees, which tether you to the soft of this earth. Emerald creeks and rosette streams bring you back to the heart of your worth.

Sounds take on new tones and hues. Angelite chords strum the sapphire blues. Emerald cadence repairs and renews, while saffron and fawn play a song of fresh dew.

Tangerine dreams and lavender beams take you out to the cusp of sunset's seam, where this world falls away and you feel the unseen. *Crystalline creams and ametrine gleams; softest peach and green tourmalines.*

Rainbows sweep with spinel beats. The heart keeps time in color's keep. And in this space of speak-less peace, all words fall away, and the world is bathed in love.

UNDER

Mango sun-streaks mix
with dragon fruit moon-
slivers: dawn is the edge
where I find day's
wonder.

Sometimes moody,
sometimes gentle,
sometimes melancholy
streams of joy; etched
with star-webbed
sunder.

Between twilight
and daylight
I find myself in the seam;
contained in her crease
all parts of me seen;
beneath sky's face
acceptance and grace,
my magical place—

There I stand wholly under.

flow

THE NATURE OF NATURE

A tree doesn't run around
shouting *I am a tree*
for all to see—
instead he simply stands
his ground, receives the seasons,
and knows his place
in this world.

A river doesn't go
against her own flow,
or fight the current of
where her streams go—
instead a river leans and
bends, allowing herself
the freedom to change
direction.

Flowers don't feel
they need to be a sea
or a cloud
or a crescent moon breeze—
instead they realize themselves
for exactly what they are, and
open, when rife, in
splendid symphony.

We can string ourselves out
into thousands of pieces
always busy doing;
live in fear and believe security
equals an amassment of stuff;
spin ourselves dizzy with
tired circles of worry—

And yet nature would teach us
the art of being, reminding:
*We were always complete
and already enough.*

ARIEL'S ARIA

Be kind to all things for through your acts of kindness you'll find all things are kind to you.

Learn to love the earth as much as your own life. Value the trees, value the ladybugs, value the snails and the seas and the slugs—they are all a part of you too.

All Creatures are an expression of Creator, and there is much you can learn from them.

Be fierce like lions. Remember lions only stalk and prey to take what they need to protect, care and love their pride.

Laugh more—like bubbling brooks—can you feel and hear their music?

Let it heal, let it heal, let it heal.

CANDLELIGHT AND COFFEE

Candles are necessity; coffee sanctuary
after a starlit walk beneath dawn's crisp—
where crescent moon becomes
my sanctity.

She bids me turn as she's want to do,
embrace my shades, my myriad hues.
Shadow-self and light-self dance
beneath the gaze of her waning glance.

Soon she'll go dark,
embracing her mysteries,
with only the stars left to guide
my dawn-time visionaries.

All roads return to yourself,
she whispers through silver wisp.

Home is the place you create in your heart,
the love that you hold is your bliss.
And I am but an echo of the
galaxies you hold within.

My mind reaches up to brush her grace,
for day is near and she'll leave me soon.
I smile at her fleeting face—

Candlelight and coffee beneath a waning moon.

THE SOUND OF SILENCE

I wonder how long
it would take,
if I were still and quiet—
(no talking,
or listening,
to anything other
than the sounds
of the birds
and the breeze
and my heart)
to become bored and
miss word's starts

and ends
and in-betweens
and conversations with others
and exchanges of meaning
and people stimulating
and connections relating
and dialogues vibrating

but for now,
too much contact
has become overwhelming
and draining,
and I yearn
(in my
introvert,
introspect
soul)
for the sound of silence
and a nervous system that's
whole

and calm
and hush
and peace,
and a brain with space to roam,
free from noise and energy leaks

I believe in the deep,
which calls in my sleep,
I would find what I need
to return to my home,
go inside
my own breath,
my own space,
my own bones

in my heart,
the thunder would roll
(shhh! listen!
can you hear its
vast roam?)
shaking and quaking
with truths unknown,
and I'd listen alone,
in silence,
and know:

I belong to the sounds
of my soul.

BEHIND CLOSED EYES

There is a time for daydream and a time to slip into the in-between. To the space of the great unknown where visions are queen, and kingdoms are built out of light-prism dreams.

Everything is possible in dream time: reality bends its knee, imagination takes stage, and whale-songs sing waves, while fancies come in on feather-pink angel wings.

You can be anybody and do anything: fly with the daffodils, talk to the mysteries, sit in the mist of Lemurian streams—create worlds out of colors, hopes and possibilities.

And you are left to wonder as you open your eyes, stare out into the vibration of physical reality: perhaps in this space of stone-songs and cat-speak, what is most real are the things only the closed eyes see.

NUCLEUS

There is peace in the breeze—
a gentle whisper of hope
for those with hearts
to listen.

Harmony in the trees—
a soft reminder of relationship:
we are stronger when
we stand connected.

Laughter in the love of a flower—
each petal an example of
the joy it strives to bring.

And consequence the lesson
of nature's interdependence—

Who we are in this world,
how we choose to treat others,
the love we withhold
or the love we give
and receive:

*Become the nucleus of choice
for the beings that we'll be.*

SECRET GARDENS

G o to secret places, especially inside of yourself. Create as often as you can, remember an act of creation can simply be a mindful exhale intended to send more kindness into the world. Stay close to nature and learn her secrets by following the whispers of the leaves and seeing where they lead.

Be a sacred rebel who listens to your own drumbeat and plays your heart of musicality constantly. *Give your imagination and your logic the same respect and accord*: both are designed for interpretive dance, weaving back and forth between the unseen and seen. Light candles and delve into giant stacks of books. Or daydream beside them and believe osmosis absorbs their energy.

Incite coziness, take cat naps, wear fuzzy socks, eat cherries on lawn's green. Chase fairies, moon gaze often, be an ambassador for radical self-belief. Ask more of your light-hopes and heart-dreams and be prepared to receive life's wild-ride prosperity.

SELENITE SOUL

She had a selenite
soul; tinged with
rings of diamonds.
Her emerald streams
ran deep; agate caves
carved drawings on
her marrow.

Her bones rattled
with ruby rocks;
her heart sealed with
larimar locks;
love was the key
that opened.

She hummed with
hymns of obsidian
blue; calcite crystals
her shards of truth.
Turquoise waves
graced her face—

And everywhere
she stepped in holy,
the stones sang her
to light.

In Nature I Belong to Myself

Nature is my friend
when nothing else is.

The hermit crab's sand-play
teases out a tired smile,
the ocean makes comfort sounds;
blue lullabies for miles.

The birds sing their hope-songs,
roosters crow with voices big,
the trees stand tall in vigilance
and say, *all is never as it seems.*

They tell me no matter how lonely
this place, I'll always find solace
in their strong embrace,
then return to the core of the
depths of true grace—

And belong to the love that is me

WEEK IN HAIKU

la luna monday
soft blues, pearls, watery feels
opalescent moon

mars governs tuesday
courageous achievement leads
ruby warrior

mercury wednesday
inventor, trickster, thinker
emerald changeling

thursday is thor's day
sapphire wisdom keeper
jupiter expands

friday for freya
love, beauty, friendship abound
diamond-like venus

saturn's saturday
limitations transmuting
obsidian pride

solaris sunday
radiant transformation
gold amber power

Care for the Sensitive Soul

No is a holy word. Use it with gratitude and reverence. Alone time is usually the only time you are 100% in your own space and energy. Protect that time fiercely.

When you are feeling tired, lost, confused, unsettled take a few moments to ground and then ask Spirit to take any energies away from you that you may be carrying, which aren't yours to carry. Go to places in nature as often as you can. Not only is it grounding, but the nature of nature is empathic, so *Mother Nature is stronger than you with the ability to hold, contain, and reflect you.*

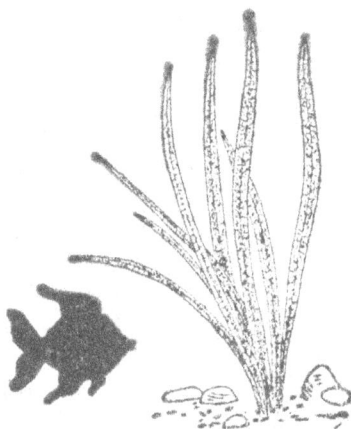

Do whatever you need to find your space of heart-quiet and still-soul. Dive into your blue often, learn to swim your seas, know that is the only way you'll truly find your truth, ebb and flow.

REALMS UNSEEN

The fairy in my rose garden
lives by the gnome in my tall palm tree,
emerald lines and verdant vines
form a gateway to their mysteries.

Where angels dance
and panthers prance
and harmony beats sublime;
in this space of magic grace
imagination reigns divine.

If this world is not for you
make up your own and visit often,
make love the law and light the key
and let your heart be softened.

Reality is what we dream and your soul
has a need for such realms unseen,
so, take refuge in what calls to you—

Let your soul be eased

EMPRESS

Empress. *Earth Mother. The Divine Feminine.* 78 cards in the tarot deck. And only one the Giver of Life.

Each time I turn her over, I stretch out my heart, reach forth, and see the love in the face of a creased, old friend.

She makes me think about what it would be to twine butterflies through my hair, soar high into the sky, transcend the lines keeping us in this space. Learn that the secret to flying is found when we yield, contract, shrink, turn in—so we can spin co-coons of shadow-selves and seek our dark-moon's face. Then emerge with the light, when day breaks from night, taking flight towards the bright on new wings of truth and grace.

She tells me to shrug off the world as I knew it. To lay down my armor and layers and shields, to sit naked in her gaze. To go to the sacred in nature, to talk to the river, to sit by the trees and rerealize, repurpose, reclaim my *life given, love driven, soul dwelling place.*

78 cards in the tarot deck. And only one the Giver of Life. The Empress she smiles with knowing eyes. An archetype of abundance; matriarchy; wise. She reminds me to gently spiral within, run free with the wind, learn the secrets of wing and hoof and fin, to trust myself down to my heart depths inside—

That there awaits my divine.

FAIRIES FLY

There are two kinds of vision that exist: the eyes and the heart, and each will have you see different things.

The eyes see what they perceive, what they can take with the limited vision of sight. But the heart sees more. It sees the miracles in front of our eyes. The truths that hide in a raindrop. The silent soliloquy of a sunrise and the symphony that crashes out new beats each day in the sea.

The heart sees love and hope, faith and dreams. It sees visions where eyes are blind. It sees beyond into worlds within worlds and intuitively knows this place is wrapped in mystery. Truth can't always be seen. Fairies fly on wings of free. Trees speak, earth breathes—

And Love wraps around it all.

STARDUST, SPRITES & INSIGHTS

Take small steps and do little things. In so doing you may just find you stepped further and went bigger than you expected.

Stay on the path when the light is bright and find a tree to rest against when things grow dark and you need some time to regroup, replenish, rejuvenate. Honor your pace of self, know it will be different than anyone else, know that's okay. Keep your mind on where you'd like to go, even as you make space for where life is creatively taking you. Include stardust and sprites in your vision.

Step lightly at times. Stride with earthquakes of love at others. Look for companions, ask for help along the way, remember you are not alone. *Keep being present for yourself.* Again, then again. Remembering that each present moment is the opportunity for a new begin.

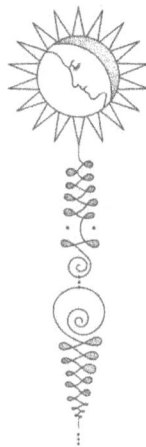

WISDOM FROM THE CAT

This life,
in all its strange glory
can be a sphinx-like
creature to love.

Whose riddles and
mysteries, lead us
into deeper wisdom,
with cat-like dexterity
by bridging polarities.

Which begs
the question
of joy's inception:
can you begin
to learn
to love
the naked skin
of now—
with all its craggy bumps
and broken imperfections?

Can you slip
into intimacy with the earth,
romanced by the trees
and flower's sweet scents.

Can you revel in their
halcyon colors and learn from
their riotous presence:

Cherry wine.
Yellow maize.
Leafy lime.
Rosy grays.
From sun up to sun set,
we evolve our soulscape's
palette every day.

In a constant evolution,
becoming Love's revolution
and Light's contribution
as we forge better ways.

Building new earth
out of hope, grace and faith.

And don't you see,
magic is found
when we realize the need
to release when, where and how
and remember—

*Joy is happening
right now.*

fLOaT
fLOW
and LeT
iT go

7
7

Emotions, Oceans & Potions

things of water, feelings, relationships and boundaries

"RIVERS KNOW THIS:
THERE IS NO HURRY.
WE SHALL GET THERE
SOME DAY."

A.A. MILNE, *WINNIE THE POOH*

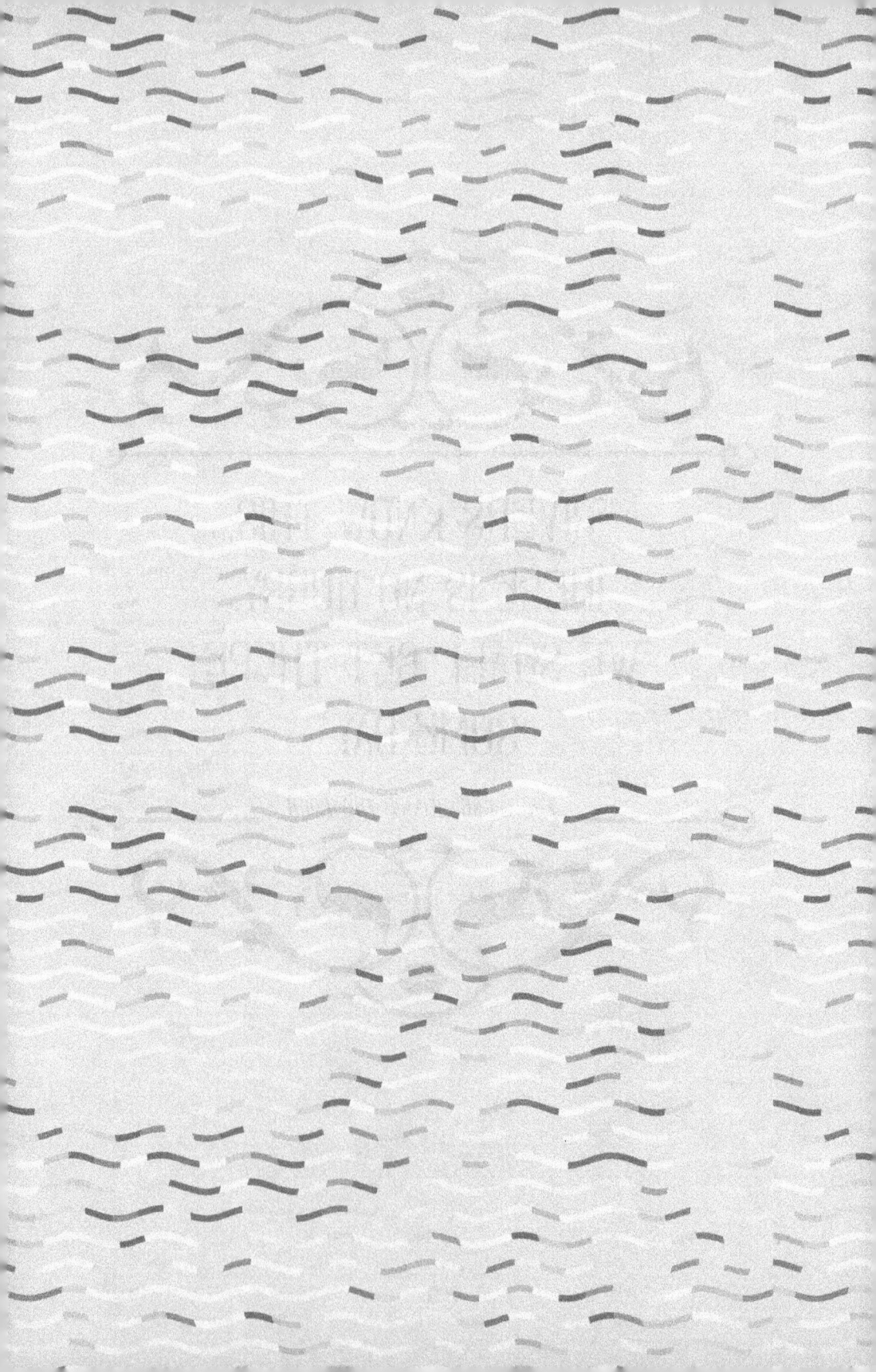

SEA > ME

I am dipping into
solitude
for the first time
in days;

like drinking water,
required at regular
intervals, lest
I dry up
and lose
love's way.

A sea of needs
and only one me;
I return to the Sea
for She's greater
than me.

Her waves hold
a message
of peace, real, and blue—
You cannot be
another's air.

You have to breathe
first for you.

WHEN SALINITY BREATHES

The ocean whispered to me of many things. How to be the cool of deep aquamarine. Whale songs and seaweed dreams.

Tempestuous truths that break against the steadfast grace of earth's shore until all that is left are shards of honesty. Poems from the deep, folded inside the creases of crab shells and scattered pieces of sea glass; lyrics of broken green, rounded by salt-brine of sea.

She tells me that somewhere inside we're all secretly mermaids, here to awaken to the divine of the mysteries. Sinking like anemone, immersion of salinity. I press my ear against her liquid sheathe: *Love, love, love she breathes.*

THE TRUTH IN A RAINDROP

the rain falls
in soft hushes;
drops tap
curvatures of
sodden lace;
rivulets stream
and pattern's
trace

truth resides
in water's life;
I in You
and You
in I;
tear maps to
the other side

within each
drop
an ocean
lays

F reedom is at the core of the energy of love. Love doesn't seek to change or entrap or bend others to be what we need. Love accepts us where we are at and allows us to be what we need to become our highest expression of self.

MIRRORS

It starts with
seeing yourself.

All sides,
flavors and melodies,
even the parts
that play
out of tune—
our discordant notes
teach us veracity:
there's truth
in all our shades.

Then it gets down
to the business
of love—
turned inwards,
grace-sourced,
& heart-towards:
there is power
and freedom
in our acts
of self-compassion.

Last it is
learning to take
that same love—
giving it outwards,
sharing in joy-pours,
paying it forwards
and knowing:

How we treat
others is always
a reflection
of how we treat
ourselves.

GAZE

Y ou can't love another into fullness. Or make them see something they do not wish to see within themselves. Or make them see YOU for the truth of who you are, when they cannot see the truth of who they are.

Or *(one of the hardest things to learn)* expect somebody else to see and love us into wholeness.

The precious mirror of relationship is one whose reflection can be easily clouded if we do not do the work of our inner world and learn to see ourselves with a clear lens. If we do not learn to recognize our external projections, so we can deal with our inner introjections. *If we do not learn to take massive amounts of responsibility for our own essence and entity.* It is only when we do this self-work that we begin to see things with crystal clarity. With compassion and grace. With a clearer gaze. We stop expecting others to be something they are not, and we start to SEE our real selves and begin to honor our authentic, deeper way.

Living life in a way where we go about the self-work of embodying, believing and seeing: that is the only way I know to truly love ourselves into wholeness of being.

flow

WE ARE THE WATER

Every time the rain falls, I find myself in her dancing drops: I in she, she in me, and together we wash things clean. Remembering life renews itself every single moment, and we are allowed to release what we don't wish to carry.

La Luna may hide her face from the night, but will soon cycle round and return with her light. Regenesis is Creation's way. Reinvention is Life's way. A sunrise resets, a good sleep reboots, our bodies shed in synchronicity as peels of our old selves fall away, while the songs in our cells bring fresh skin to dew.

We are transformative creatures, and this is a transient place. We can be baptized in a blink. Birth ourselves again. Restart, reconstruct, relinquish, review. Every day we are the water which rinses this world new.

The rain how she falls, I in she, she in me. Together we tap dance in crystalline streams—*toe heel tip // tap tap tap // love is all // slap heel dig*—making art with her drops on the ground, down the streets.

We go hand and hand washing everything clean.

flow

Words for Empaths

We are about different things in this world, and the trick is to fig-
ure out *those who are what you are about, and those who aren't.*
Then learn to meet people where they are at in accordance with your own
boundaries of self-love.

Not everybody is meant to get the best of our heart. We can love fierce-
ly while still allowing only those who are willing to love fierce back into
our inner sanctums: *we can't carry everybody in that space.*

That's the rub of being an empath or highly sensitive, because at some
point, most empaths have tried to engage in their relationships from the
deepest point of their heart center, believing that others are engaging with
the same equity and love. Yet not everybody is in that space in this life, and
that is where our wisdom and discernment must come in

*Allow people to be where they are at, and they will show you exactly where
they are at.*

Don't waste time trying to change them or trying to do their heart work
for them. Just pay attention as you go on affirming and being who you
are, so you don't take on their energy or confuse their way of being in the
world for your way of being in the world.

Then we get to make self-loving and self-honoring choices about how
we want to navigate that relational space. Continuously empowering our-
selves to keep walking our path and working on the only heart-light we
truly can.

A SHORT STORY ON FLIGHT

when she
reached high
to dream the sky,
she left behind
her mind's confines,
flying the seas
on silver wings,
until she chimed
the ring
of angel
sing,

and in those
moments
of harmony,
she swam
her soul's
complete

PISCES DREAMS

goldfish clouds;
pisces dreams;
fluid, floating freeing—

a girl by the sea;
hermit crab breeze;
easy, playful, being.

in and out, the ocean's song—
let it go
live to love
learn to see.

harmony's
the path to peace,
and first it starts *in me.*

Rain Days

Rain days are like blankets.
Meant to be curled into with gentle soliloquy.
An invitation to travel to the worlds in-between
Where angels dance unknown with wild creativity.

Behind the veil mysteries await.
Love is the portal to travel this space.
The life of a raindrop is a story of change and grace.
When we allow life to shape us magic takes place.

And we, like the rain, become more—
An out-pour of peace on a thirsty ground

LOVING KINDNESS MEDITATION

Don't assume other people are broken. Or need to be fixed. Or want to be fixed. Or that you know what's right or best for their life.

The only assumption that is fair to make is the assumption that as a fellow human being they have their own soul path, and they are walking that path as best they know how. Subject to mistakes and learning by trial and error, getting lost and wandering in the wilderness, falling into holes then getting back up then rising, redirecting and renavigating—just as you are.

Learning to compassionately detach and make space to let another go their own way is one of the harder lessons we have to learn in life. And yet, it makes all the difference when it comes to our own peace of mind and peace of heart. We can choose to get sucked into another's story and drama, or we can choose to free ourselves and trust life to help them work it out.

Sometimes the best gift you can give yourself is to practice releasing somebody with loving kindness. *May you be safe, may you be well, may life guide you as you need.*

Then turn that beautiful blessing back around on yourself. *May I be safe, may I be well, may life guide me as I need.*

Then remember, even when our physical paths diverge, we are still connected at the source where it counts, and Life is big enough to know our hearts and meet each of us exactly where we are at. *May we be safe, may we be well, may life guide us as we need.*

The Art of Flow

Learn to flow in the direction life leads. See disappointments as opportunities. Feel the real of all feels involved, then honor how you'd like to feel. Take steps to move in that direction, write your affirmations in the stars.

Find the artistry in the seemingly broken. Find the luck in the seeming unlucky. Find the possibility for upcycling and creativity. Adjust your flow so you go at the pace of ease and love; allow all else to sow then flow from those.

Mermaid often. Practice self-compassion. Make friends with the sea.

Create disturbing beauty by finding the beauty in spaces others dismiss or discard. Start that process within yourself. Learn to receive from the energy of day. Keep empowering yourself to live a life where love is your radiant wealth.

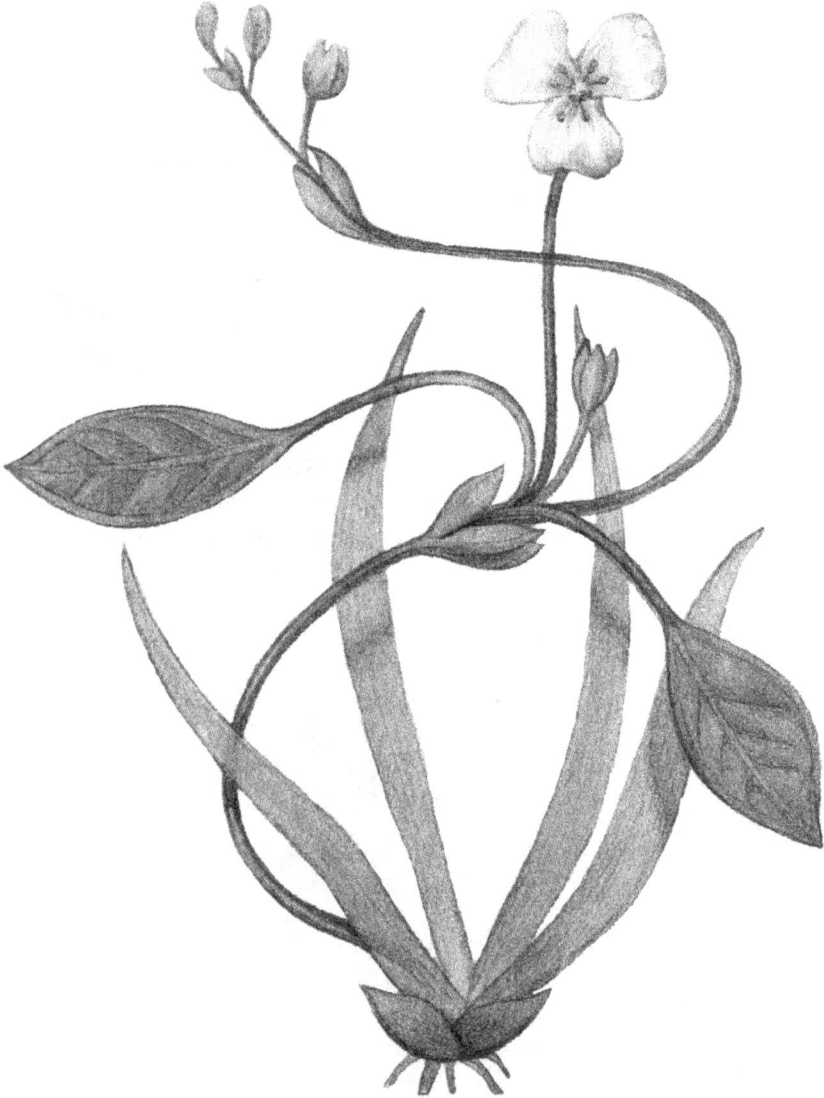

SEAWEED DANCE

tangled up in green—
emerald
forest
kelly
moss
a spray of
beryl mist

I let myself drift…
content to be
with my friends
in the marine,
and the mermaids
of blue's sink,
and the plants
of ocean's drink

wrapped around me
they anchor me
to the sea.

drawing me
inwards
and under
and down
—I nestle in the deep
float with the green—
keeping time
keeping love
keeping soft
keeping hope

free to be
no one but me,
I swim and joy
and dance with
sea's mysteries

Hard Days

I want to say
life is the seam
where sky meets soft,
and I fold myself into
her cusp when it's gray;
But our world's reaching
out in the thick of that seam,
and these have been
hard days.

I want to say
we live in a place
where we fight to bare heart
instead of bear arms;
and we care for the earth
and her burden of strain;
But so many are blind
to love's wisened ways,
and these have been
hard days.

Apocalyptic –
misogynistic –
sadistic –
cataclysmic –
the shatter is felt
to the depths of our veins.

And we're awakened
and shaken
and forced to arrange,
our perspectives on life
and humanity's ways,
as we learn to see truth
in the hard of
these days.

I want to say
life is the palms
and the sway of
the breeze that greeted
my day—

But my heart
cries out against the breaks
stretches for light in the face
of dark's place;
stands at the cusp of
humanity's change,
and prays for *Love*
in the heart of
these days.

Rain Dance

There were these days
where I wanted to
cry over all of it.

Cry for the beauty,
cry for the ache,
cry for the wounds of the past
cry for the hope of the future.

Cry with the rain
outside, echoing down;
her drops living water
for a tired, thirsty ground.

We'd dance together
in fluid harmony,
tears intermingled,
watery weaves.
One mind, one heart, one plea
among our sodden cheeks. . .

Peace.
Peace.
Peace.
Please.

Taps

She speaks to me,
in a whisper,
the gentle mother
of this island.

Of times passed by,
of days to come,
and the future
of our times.

She tells me love
will be the choice
that directs the course
of history.

Humanity
determined by
the light or dark
we choose to be—

Day is done,
sun is gone,
from the lake,
from the hills,
from the sky;
all is well,
safely rest,
God is nigh.

She breathes out peace
Aloha au ia ʻoe,
she beats,
while the rain plays *Taps*
and softly weeps.

*original words from "Taps" by Horace Lorenzo

Grief's Doorway

Honoring our grief is not about focusing on what we've lost—not at all. It's about our relationship with our self and our relationship with life. It's about making space to remember what matters most: *the love we give and the love we are in this place.* It's about creating opportunity to grow in relationship and connection with the world around us.

Our losses are doorways to a greater space of remembering, appreciating, releasing, loving, grieving, and growing. We are reminded of our true nature when we honor: *we are not separate, we are connected to everything, our past and present continually weaving together to unfold the mystery of our future.*

Honoring is about giving ourselves permission to be our full selves. To feel our full selves. To feel the full scope of our lives, which includes our losses. To honor our process of being, our unique relationship to grief and loss and love, our own trail of being a true human.

We honor so we keep resolving, dissolving, evolving our relationship with life. We honor because we have loved, and in so doing we discover that love is grief's antidote.

It Comes in Waves

In waves and cycles and endless shades and tones: *healing is a friend who appears when we need it most.*

Not linear, but cyclical, not absolute, but transitional—meeting us exactly where we are at when it's time to grow beyond the physical. And though we may not always recognize it as such, disruptions in heart and emotional consciousness are opportunities for widening soul's cognizance.

So, we can keep growing into the full of heart's resonance and mending our seams through love's consonance.

SEA SECRETS

The sea, she is a mystery.

Unfathomable in reach,
incomprehensible in belief,
her darkest depths hold
secrets that yet no eyes
have seen.

She'll sing you a
song in the morning,
a lullaby with noon's
gentle tide,
then bid you to sleep
with a ballad of waves
to the rhythm of
full moon's light.

She'll take your
secrets in her stead,
hold them in
her keep—
and still her flows
will come and go,
wash your lines
into her sweep
…until you forget
where you end
and she begins…

She is a mystery, the sea.

Flux

Balance is nothing if not obtainable—each time you find equilibrium, life comes along and changes you with its strokes.

Peace is finding your fish in the flow. By learning to swim *upstream, downstream in-between the streams* of life's dynamic ebbs and grows.

Stability is but an illusion of control—for elasticity, plasticity and reactivity always move with rapidity following the ebb of a slow.

These shifting days where snow meets green; new drops of blue tuck into each changeful, sacred pause—

I keep tripping on my mutability, then finding peace within my flux.

WHALES

Down in the deep, deep blue, they speak to you, and I. Harbingers of light, bridging realms only seen in the mind. Messengers of harmony, they teach us to live aligned. *To be mindful of our ripple effects and aware that our acts impact other lives.*

Wisdom-keepers, current-seekers, ocean-drinkers, migrant-thinkers, whose intelligence cannot be defined. They were here before time, have seen all with Great Eyes, and know each drop, drip, and wave that has ever transpired. Ancient Sages of the deep. Ocean Angels keep. They weep and leap and seep their weaves and help our souls inspire belief.

Down in the deep, deep blue, they speak to I and you. Awakening the sentient streams of universe's truth. A harmonic, symphonic of sonorous hues. And if you listen carefully, you'll hear their whale-song blue:

Keep listening for us child, for we wait to speak to you.

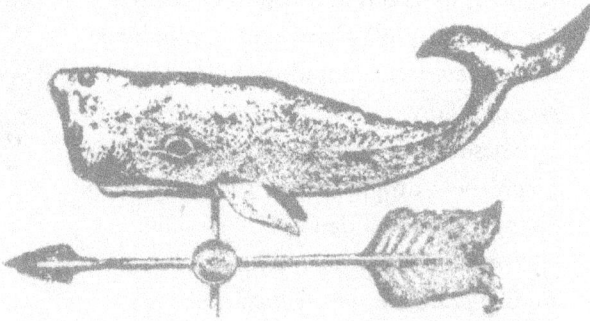

ONE STEP CLOSER

The ocean will tell you
there are no perfect tides.

We let life shape
and change our shores,
with ragged waves
and crooked lines.

Each one of us flailing,
then swimming, then floating,
and finding our way
in our seas.

Moving towards light
—*in all its vast forms*—
and learning to sink
in our mysteries.

Each pearl retrieved
from our own depths
teaching us how to make peace—

And what we don't realize
is when we love ourselves,
we are one step closer
to divinity.

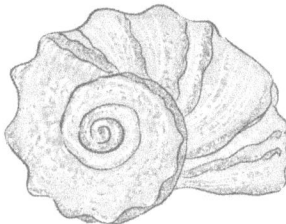

PALETTE OF WHOLENESS

Feelings run deep.
You can weep
rivers of gray grief
underneath
a sunny disposition
of joy,
and hold both
experiences in equity.

You can live
the picture
that is you right now,
embrace each day's green,
even as part of you
travels by sea,
searching for
blue's missing piece.

You can unfold
your red rose in bloom,
and bask in the
beauty of your own breathing,
even as lotus
sinks deep in the
brown mud, embracing
the grit that comes with being.

Subconscious
submergence sinks,
as illumined
awareness thinks,
and somewhere in
the space between
our colors link—
and we create a new palette
of wholeness.

THE ILLUSION

sea salt speaks
brine lines rhyme,
poetry in motion

stretching wide
her waves collide,
boundaries dissolution

she is me
and i am sea,
a drop inside her ocean

love ties all binds
through space and time,
separation is an illusion

PAINT THE SKY WITH STARS

We aren't meant to walk somebody else's path for them, and that can be a really tough truth to take.

It's not that any of us necessarily want to try and walk somebody else's path—most of us have enough going on with our own. It's more that when we care about people, we want good things for them. We want to see them flourish, grow, and be happy and free. When we want those things for the people we love, and when they make decisions that harm or hurt, it is rough to be the bystander.

That's usually the point we want to jump off our path, hop onto theirs, and try to steer them in the "right" direction.

When that happens repeatedly and chronically, we will eventually lose ourselves in our efforts. Lose our own hopes and dreams. Lose where our path ends and theirs begins. Lose our own sense of self.

So, if we can't walk their path what can we do?

We can pray for others. Send light, hope for healing, and ask that life support them. We can put the intention out into the ether that we desire whatever is for their highest good. We can encourage. We can love—sometimes up close, and sometimes from afar, depending on what boundaries necessitate.

We can hold space, keep believing in them, and keep believing life is full of miracles and love can bring about redemptive change. We can release them to the universe if we recognize we're no longer meant to be a space holder for them and know that the universe is absolutely big enough to support them.

We can work on ourselves. Work on our own path. Get busy cultivating what we see on that path. Pruning the trees, planting roses, learning the language of bunnies, clouds, and grass, so we receive nature's healing qualities and learn to go deeper within.

We can look for the places where our path feels dark and work on painting the sky with stars, so we always have something to navigate by. We can stand—exactly where we are at—and send love backward and forward on our own timeline. Trusting it to reach our younger self and future self, bringing hope, mending, and integration.

We can work on nourishing what is inside of us: our heart, our thoughts, our breath, our feelings, our gratitude, and our stories. We can do the work of self. We can trust that if we do this, we will be so full of life and love, we can stay on our own path and shine our love light so bright that it casts a glow onto others, *encouraging them to find what they need to meet their own requirements of soul.*

Let the Shadows Fall Behind You

Letting go is not for the faint of heart. After all, not everyone can defy sorrow by turning their face to the sunlight, still choosing joy despite their knowledge of the night.

Not everyone can release broken dreams on golden wings of days gone by, steeling their gaze towards ocean's soft forgiving lines, which serve to remind—be in the bliss-flow of the now, as only love endures; all else will pass in time.

And not everyone can take a broken heart, smashed against life's shores of hard-chipped pain, and rebuild it into something bigger than before... restitched, reworked, reformed, repieced with love's unending gains.

So, if you happen to find yourself in such a space, where life is asking you to relinquish, release, and trust in its unknown grace. Then remember the scope of your brave, remember the truth of where you came, and know that all we release will come round in new way, each fleeting beat of life's sweet well worth any bitter tang—

In the place where grief and love meet: your heart will mend again.

WATER WISDOM

I don't know how to feel less; I only know how to feel everything and give it back to fluidity's whole. Each drop and trickle and tributary flow—water has a wisdom all her own.

She knows when to ebb and when to return to tide. Worlds within worlds, she holds a universe inside. Stormy seas, calm ponds, river breeze and ocean's brine. She wears a million faces from the darkest to the light.

Emotions are fluid, so are we, and so is life. Tears sanctify. Rains baptize. Sweat purifies. Streams heal. A shower can rinse the day away or help shed the worn skins of who, what and how you no longer wish to feel.

Who says we have to be the same from one moment to the next? As if we don't each have our own profundity of sea; or the capacity to yearn to grow into bigger creatures of beauty; or mermaid hearts who ring with sapphire bells—urging us down towards the plunge of our deep.

And like the sea, so do we, hold the mysteries we seek. When we dive into our possibility of being and *redeem, renew, release.*

Asilomar Sea-dreams

gray sea speaks
of tempestuous
ease;
the kind of flow
where we allow
our cares to
become streams

...of watery blue
and ripply marine—
life can be a choppy ride,
yet we can learn
to follow
its leans

find grace for
the rip curls,
the wave whirls,
the azurite seams—
let love be the water
which cleans
our laborite
seas

and brings our
soul-murmurings
back to an equilibrium
of peace.

bE liKE
thE brEEzE
iN EasE

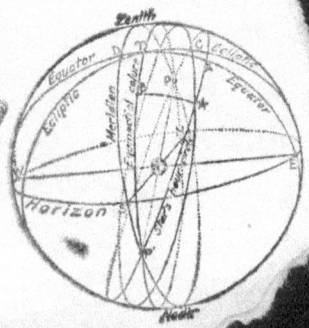

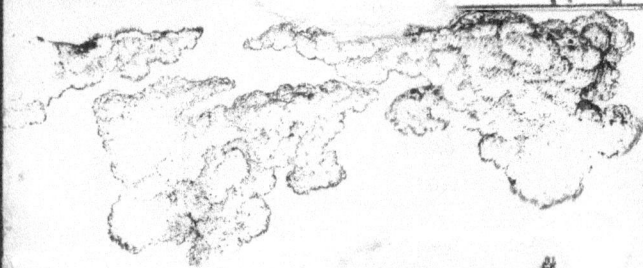

Trees, Transitions
&
Transfigurations

things of time, truth, self and soul

'It doesn't happen all at once,' said the Skin Horse. 'You become. It takes a long time. That's why it doesn't happen often to people who break easily, or have sharp edges, or who have to be carefully kept. Generally, by the time you are Real, most of your hair has been loved off, and your eyes drop out and you get loose in the joints and very shabby. But these things don't matter at all, because once you are Real you can't be ugly, except to people who don't understand.

Margery Williams Bianco, *The Velveteen Rabbit*

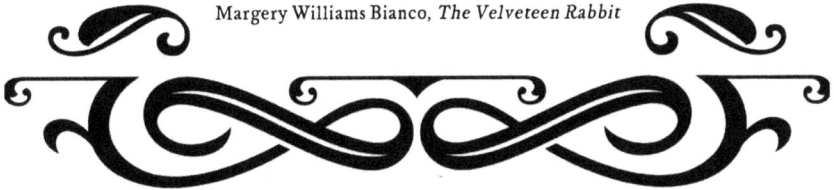

Tree-isms

Find a tree and lean on its wisdom, and it will teach you how to be part of the is-dom: *Where just being is an act of sacred creativity. Observation becomes the art of curious discovery.*

Reminding us life never shakes out the way that we think, and we'll lose the joy of day if we don't stop and blink—And take it in, the magic of the now. Because magic is always happening, it's just a matter of how.

So, instead of trying to figure it out, or force it, or effort away in unceasing kowtow: Be like a tree. Present, aware, and open to receive. The magic all around that's found—when we simply trust, still, and allow.

SEAMS

I am continuing
to learn that
most of life is
experienced
in the seams
of in-between.

Because by the time
we arrive
where we believed
we wanted to go—

*Something new
has already unfolded
and is ushering us
into the unknown.*

It's a strange moon—
like dance of tension,
where we're continually
releasing
and receiving
to keep shedding
yet stepping
into soul's
fullest growth.

Letter to a Young Dancer
from a Poet

I know they are but words to you.
Words and *chainé*
and *ál a seconde*
and point your toes in the middle section.
And sweat on a Thursday night when your homework is due
and your phone has 20 messages awaiting return
and the dog needs to be fed
—and you're at dance class instead.

      But to me, they are a pivot.

The night my brother died.
An ugly flexed foot, sudden turn, out of line.
Where life was danced in reverse.
180 from the direction
I thought I was supposed to go,
was supposed to be,
was supposed to find.

I had to make a choice in my pain
about the path I'd choose to wind—
(words are my taps, my rhythms, my flaps)
and so, I wrote that poem for you
about the choices we make in our lives.

I know they are but words to you,
how many times have you heard them—
we become the love we give
we become the love we give
we become the love we give
But it's true. We do. I did. You Will.

Become the love you give
every second of your life—
each act, deed and thought shaping
your soul,
your heart,

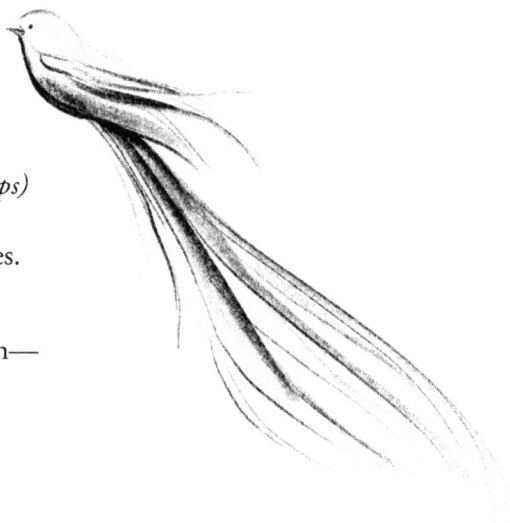

85

your steps,
your soles,
    the calluses on your feet don't lie,
    telling a story of hard work, choice and time.
    I stood in ballet class once too
    black leo, pink tights, straight spine
      plié…
        plié…
          grand plié…

Until my knees flexed, my legs stretched, my feet ached.
And dance will force you to learn to dig deep,
become the strength, heart, and grace you carry inside.

Thursday night I was watching you,
at rehearsal, the girl in the blue,
did you know those were my words
that mine is the face behind the lines and rhymes?
to a dance you've danced dozens of times.

      But to me, they are my blistered toes.

My *jeté* with a battle cry.
My unexpected floor work
and shuffle ball change
and being the kid in the back of the line—
who's awaiting recognition,
then learns, *who cares where you are put?*
just dance your truth wherever you find yourself:
go be a light and shine.

Because life is way too short
to squander your gifts of joy and bright.
And each time you dance, you step, you act—
you make a choice
about who'll you'll be in this time.

I know they are but words to you,
(it's your stage now, you're young, this is your time.)
But I move
leave this place
leave this floor
leave this space
in only 3 months-time.
Pack up my tap shoes, say goodbye, then find a new place in line,
(a piece of me will always remain, fare thee well studio 49.)

So, this is my inner poet talking to you as I sit and write these rhymes.
A dancer too, I was once like you, and will leave with this advice:
Point your toes.
Go to ballet class.
Stretch your splits, souls, and kicks, and practice your acro tricks.
And please, show up for rehearsal on time.

Be your brightest dancing fools,
yet don't take the outcome so seriously—
whoever you'll be, you'll become the love you need.
And know in the end the real dance
is who you choose to be in this life.

THE RELUCTANT SHAMAN

Nobody who is called to this path
wants to walk it.

It is not for the faint of heart
or thin of skin
or the ones who seek ease or acceptance
or those who'd stall when soul gives call.

It comes at a cost
—a ripping of your seams—
(and maybe more than once, two times,
three times, *so many times I've lost count*)
so Life can keep taking you apart
and make the room to stretch your heart.

Teach you about what is real.
Teach you the mystery of change.
Sweep you up into a city of clouds
where you see the darkness, the burning, the hurting, the pain—
see the great need
for peace
for healing
for love
in the staunched flow of humanity's veins.

You'll be bade to go down deep,
find your pearls amongst dark sediment,
charged to face your shadow selves
and learn the grace of penitence.
There but the grace of love go I
these words become your catechist,
and you can't be anything but true—
fierce authenticity your regiment.

You will find yourself to lose yourself.
Learn to become to be undone.
And just when you've reached a stasis of place,
Life will ask you to leave that comfort zone,
pack up your heart to learn new space.

I wouldn't wish this path on anyone,
it is some of the loneliest steps I ever walked.

And yet I have many guides, unseen by the eyes,
the trees are my friends and my spirits the sky,
I see the love laced web connecting
You—and all that lays between—and I.

So, reluctant steps with faithful bent
(you really can't ignore the insistent soul's intent)
I keep stepping towards the light.

Moss Symphonies

If you talk to a tree for a while, you'll learn a great deal about patience and perspective. What it means to withstand storms and seasons and change, to endure strong and unchanged, even as you let the face of life weather you and teach you to bend, *so you will not break.*

Archives of history, trees know things people have forgotten.

How to live in unity and harmony. How to only take up as much space as one needs. How to grow the kinds of roots, not easily felled, respecting the humble nature of earth's sacred soil. How to talk to the sky and listen and make friends with the creatures who shelter 'neath and near. *How to be connected to everything around you, yet retain your own essence, unique and clear.*

Storytellers, one needs to know how to read their books, each tree telling a tale through mahogany rings and chocolate bark and verdant visage. Akashic Keepers of wisdom, their amber eyes remind: *slow down, breathe, do no harm, be kind.* There is a reason walking in the forest comes with its own sense of holy sublime. Moss symphonies play as olive branches sway, and pine green light soothes with ancient hymns of love's divine.

Listen closely to songs so hallowed they have the power to sanctify a heart's insides: *This is what it means to be real, this is what it means to be whole, this is what it means to live fully alive*

WISDOM RHYTHMS

The jungle breeze
she comforts me,
reminds me it's
enough to be—

In the moment
with this green,
trusting things
to unfold at the seam

Of hopes, dreams
and possibilities—
mixed with vision
and intent and
wise energy.

Who knows that
like the trees, we
also grow and leaf;
a continual shedding
of last season's
sleeves.

We can't grow anew
if we won't let ourselves
unform and undo,
from gold
to rust
to bare
to bud
to spring
to green—

So, the best we can do
is listen to the rhythms,
learn to be a keeper
of our own wisdom—

And know we are always
moving in the direction
of our highest protection
and soul-growth.

You Are the Universe

I know this is
a hard one
(it's hard for me too)—
but sometimes we
have to *trust* in our own
higher plan for self.

You are part of this
universe, are you not?

An equal participant in
this time
and this space.
You help speak your life
into being each day—
the lights of one
trillion orbs of stardust are
running through your veins.

You are here.
You have purpose.
You are powerful.
You matter.

My dear one,
from time to time
everybody loses their way,
but though we can't always see
the mysteries,
we can choose to believe
in the power of *Self*—

Keep learning to be
the light that we seek.

KEYS

There are those days where you just have to be.

Be with your restless stillness and your half-formed knowings. Be in the rain, the breeze, the sun, and sink into the soft rhythms of nature which never rush their own process of change. Instead, changing exactly when it is time in small increments and then giant bursts of blooming seed.

Yesterday is behind us, and tomorrow is still out of reach. What we have is now and this present moment of being in our own mysteries. Then learning to recognize the keys to unlocking the *self*, which life brings into our path when it's time for greater clarity.

Keys don't always arrive in grand ways. More often than not they come in small clues and cues—bits and pieces of feelings, scraps of words, soft signs and subtle nudges, slight erosions and quiet reshapings. The constancy of nightfall and the break of each new day, which reminds us life moves towards perpetual motion, growth, change, and prosperity. *A deepening vocabulary of our own golden soul-sing and heart-speak.*

If you are in the abyss, or have fallen between the cracks, or would like to know but don't see how—allow yourself this pause and breath and beat. And know it simply isn't time for clearer seeing. You'll see when you see. No sooner and no later.

In the meantime: Tread gently. Whisper often to yourself. Make it the softest of soft. Hold a warm mug of amenity. Nestle into comfort rituals. Breathe with the trees and listen to their songs of wholeness. Give yourself this space and time.

Quit trying to be the shaper. Be the shapee.

Most of all, just be. Trust beyond. Open your heart to life's myriad keys. Knowing that when it's the right moment, the answers you seek will unlock and become seen.

NEW

There is something
about the word *new*
that encourages
crisp hope and our desire
for better.

New season,
new month,
new cycle,
new year—

*We send our dreams
for new up into the sky
tied with tails of fairy
dust and starlight.*

Our wishes for our lives
create our pathways
of decision, and
our dreams can only
be as big or small as
we envision.

We cannot stop the
turn of time,
but we can embrace
the change of these days,
each step forward
a step closer to:

*New hope.
New love.
New truth,
New ways.*

Rhythms & Seasons

Not all seasons look the way we think they should unfold and be. Golden, grief-laden autumn can play a song on our inner heart-sleeves, while outside spring birds chirp riotously on newly blossomed green-leaves.

Winter can catch us off guard on a summer's day, if we're in a snowy season of life-break or heart-ache, even while surrounded by sunshine ways and bluebird haze.

We can quicken during earth's deep freeze. Plant seeds when the ground is still laced with ice brandy. Begin to bloom during harvest, when the rest of the earth is ready to reap and sleep.

Moon faces and tide phases teach us the cyclical nature of our own inner spaces. Each heart-beat and feel-speak and soul-seek spiraling us towards our cosmic-peak. Those inner mountains we climb where we can gaze out and see the bigger picture of our place in the whole. *Ascending, descending, and transcending— again and again—as we move towards a greater sense of our full.*

Letting life's grains of sands rub, twist, and grist us into opaline pearls. Allowing the universe within to shift, drift, and lift, as we peace-wink and faith-blink and love-think about who we are becoming in this world.

LEVITY'S GRAVITY

It's found on
the crest
of the cusp:
balance,
that tension
between
not taking it
so seriously
(even Buddha
with his rolling
belly knew
that those who
seek laughter—
seek *truth*
seek *love*
see *god*)
all while
embracing with
tender ferocity,
this brief
gift that
is our
life.

Cartwheels & Spirals

Take soft and gentle moments for yourself as often as you need. There are many things that will blow you off course in this world, so you have to learn how to find safe harbor: *Safe being those spaces where acceptance, comfort, and grounding prevail.*

Know what you are about, even as you give yourself room to not know and grow. There is a tension between knowing and unknowing whose threads weave new colors and patterns into the synapses of our tapestry.

Make a little space for those times life becomes circumvoluted, and the bigger picture spirals. Life is not linear, so sometimes the best we can do is cartwheel in the air and find levity and perspicacity when we look at the world sideways, trusting we'll find new footing once we land.

Don't mistake other's opinions for truth or anything other than a reflection of their inner world. You'll find the more well-organized the heart, the less the judgment, and the more space for grace.

Above all else, just keep being present for yourself. Show up, listen up, love up: learn to embody you. For only in your fullness and richness of self, will you find what you need to hold your own hand, stay on your path, see yourself through, and keep on walking your truth.

MESSAGE FROM THE BAMBOO

The bamboo will clack and cling and swing from side to side. The willow will sway in the breeze knowing to lean in the direction the wind rides. And so too, must we learn to bend with life's shifting tides.

Finding flexibility, adaptability, and creativity in the mystery of being. Wandering around with a mystic's heart, who is always open to greater seeing. *Testing patterns and what we think we know, so we can keep staying open to new believing.*

Branches, who are brittle break, because they resist life's weight. They don't know how to let their limbs limbo to limber with life's changeful state.

Attach too hard to outcome, and you'll be chronically disappointed.

Refuse to see all parts of yourself, and your inner world will feel dark and disjointed.

Believe you know the only path to the heart, and your vision won't be anointed.

Stay open and clear, yet humble in love, and the way will then be appointed.

By the grace of life, who helps us bend with the winds of the forest of change. Just like the bamboo we must become, continually growing and changing our shape.

Metamorphosis

There are times in our life where change happens suddenly. A lightning bolt moment will crack us wide open, and we never see it coming. But more often than not, change happens in degrees, gradations, and tones. Life's ocean slowly erodes and reshapes our soul-shore. We respond with subtle variations of intention and thought that gradually lead to new patterns and shades in our palette. After a while, those shades become a part of us, and we realize we've integrated new ways of being, and in so doing, *we've created space for more change.*

So, don't be discouraged if you feel like you're not moving as fast as you think you should. Or you've been trying to transform and find the nature of your own metamorphosis has taken place throughout many seasons instead of one swift swoop. Or if you feel like you should have *healed* or *empowered* or *improved* yesterday, and you don't think you're far enough along today.

Just offer yourself up to the waters of life and trust your heart-terrain is exactly where it needs to be in the change. Then think of one small tangible thing you can do to support your personal palette of growth and move in that direction.

Into the Woods

We need to go into the woods of our soul often. Exploring the heart of our own forest and finding our soul's secret gifts. We have worlds within worlds inside of ourselves—waiting to reveal their holy mysteries—when we carve out space to go within.

Going inwards is how we better learn to listen; it helps us to slow down and be intentional about our relationship with our self. Going inwards is a mindful act where we can explore the flora and the fauna of the self. The more we do this, the more we notice our shifts, witness our changes, and begin to learn the language of our soul's cycles, ebbs, and flows.

If we are seeking to live life from an authentic, intuitive space, then *our experience of self is going to be the experience most helpful to us.* Being in touch with our experience of self requires a great deal of self-awareness gained through reflecting, listening, observing, discovering, exploring, and learning our own personal language.

It is only through knowing ourselves that we develop discernment and wisdom regarding our process. When we go inside, we begin to see our inner world is crackling with information and saturated with intelligence. Going within helps us tap into our soul wisdom and find the essence of our life force, which sustains, grows, and nourishes us.

The more we learn to spend time with and within ourselves, the more we grow our relationship with our inner earth. We learn the nuances of our soil, notice the way our seasonal patterns play out, and we pay attention to the ebbs and flows within and how those interplay with the exterior world.

We find our natural rhythms. We find our intuitive cycle. We learn to listen. We want to learn our truth.

All of that is what living soulfully is about. Trusting the world within, letting our own voice be our guide, and leading heart-based lives of believing in our own soul process, which is invisible, but utterly real.

TREE TONES

It occurs to me,
that just like
the trees,
so too do we
need to learn
how to breathe.
And let ourselves
be whatever
we'll be,
trusting our process
of gravidity.
Knowing we'll
cycle as many times
as we need,
and rebirth
ourselves into
fuller brevity.
Growing then
leafing;
reaching,
and breathing—
so, too do we
become like
the trees.

CATCH AND RELEASE

My dear one,
it is a brave, big world
if you let it.
Filled with scopes
that collide in our nights,
filled with lights
that multiply our scopes.

Each one of us
a jubilation
of kinetic creation
(a soul's evolution)
told in the tales
of each personal
revelation.

We keep waiting
for a destination,
but the time
to live,
to breathe,
to be
is Now.

We can't realize
the truth found
in existence
without learning
to sink into sound

and touch, and taste,
and sense, and breath,
and love, and you—
and me.

My dear one,
you have been
called here
to live,
to feel,
to learn to see.

Each day a
variegated dance
of catch and release,
a journey of
discovery
intensity
tenacity
epiphany—

So, you can learn the truth
of what it means
to BE.

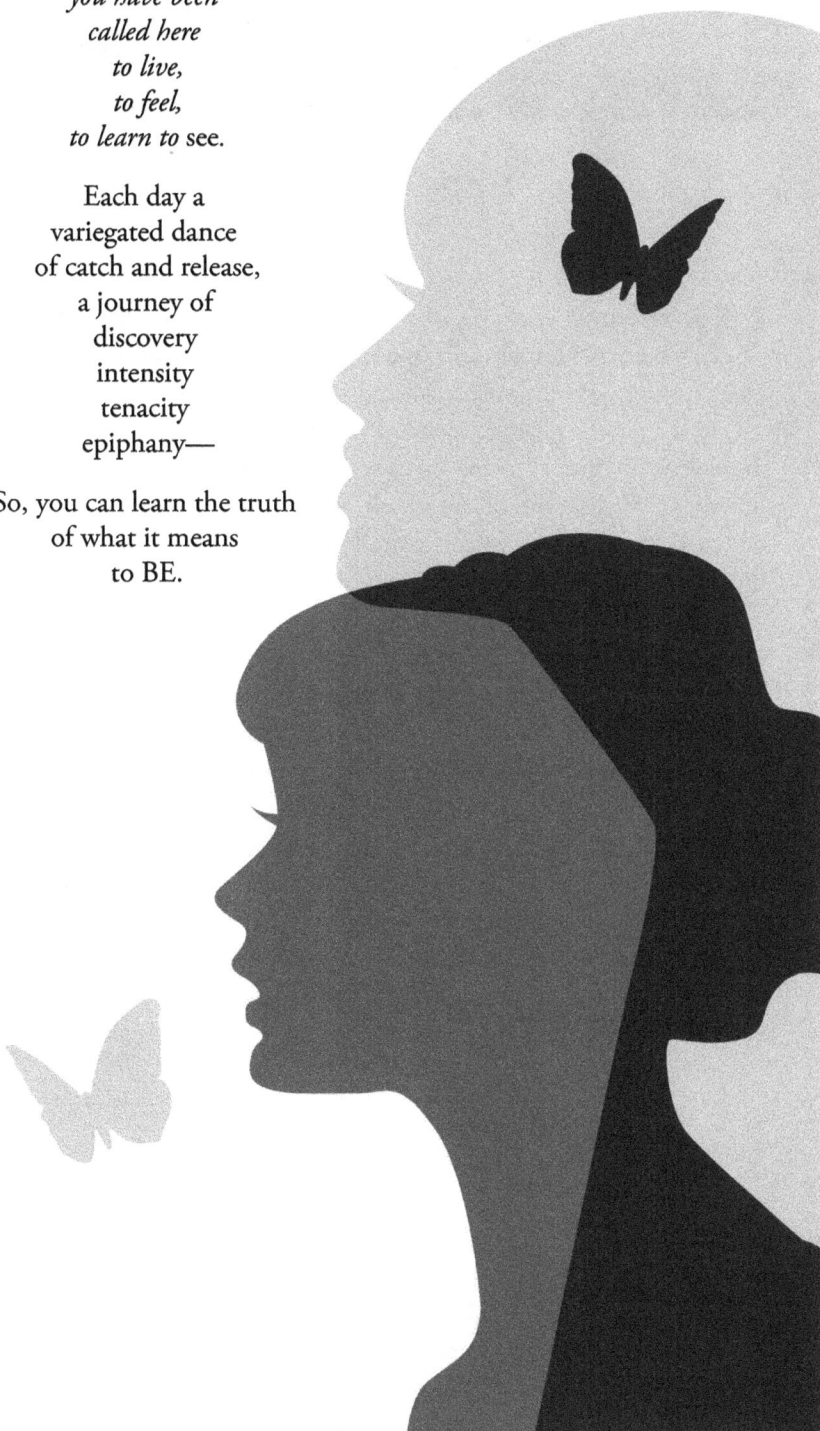

Soul Retrieval

We recover ourselves in bits and pieces. A push of momentum here. A moment of hope over there. A flash of transcendence raises us up and over our breaks and spillage and grief.

For a minute we are suspended on feathered wings lifting us above the bigger picture; allowing us to see our whole. Giving us time to fly down and retrieve the pieces of self we laid or dropped along the way, taking back anything we accidentally gave away. Reclaiming parts we didn't even know we'd lost. Reintegrating aspects long forgot.

Recovering, recalling, rewiring, renewing. Collecting fragments of psyche and soul, which help compose a deeper completion.

Remembering: *if this world doesn't work for you then you've got to rework your world.* Sewing wings of clarity and fortitude, so you can go on a treasure hunt for your truth. Learning that so much of what glitters will not turn out to be your gems or your gold, but you will surprise yourself with how many diamonds you find in the rough of your soul. You will surprise yourself with what you collect upon the way, and where your truest treasure grows.

You will surprise yourself with your own capacity for wingspan and flight; becoming fuller with each descent and ascent, as you continue to move in your direction of light.

NEW WINGS

I t's easy to talk about being the change, but to actually *change* is a different thing entirely.

In part, because the work of change is arduous, aching, and decidedly unglamorous. There is little initial appeal in emptying the contents of one's life for careful scrutiny outside of your own conviction you've had enough of the old ways and are willing to take responsibility for new ways—*and if you have such a conviction, listen to it.*

The process of real change is day to day. It is time in the trenches challenging your behaviors, thought-life, habits, relational patterns and emotions. It's the release of pretending you've got it all under control. It's a commitment to doing things differently and then doing the work.

Nobody can do this work for you. It is your decision, your accountability to hold yourself to better standards, your responsibility to oversee your work. Work lacking in glory because it occurs inside, and there is little validation initially for such tiresome, internal tasks.

But if you stick with it, the validation will come. Possibly from others but by that time it truly won't matter. For you will have found that in the process of changing your life, you have fallen in love with your own life and vision, and you will have claimed your life with such beautiful embodiment that you will never go back to the way things were before.

You cannot fit a butterfly who is busy flying free back into its cocoon of smaller things. For it will have grown much too wild to want to do anything but keep shedding, letting, and spreading its new wings.

Sacred Hoops

Separate yet connected,
each of us is a sacred hoop
within a hoop, within a hoop.

The universe speaking in
circles and cycles, bringing us
back around to our truth.

Holiness is found in each breath,
dust in our veins and stars in our skin,
deepest purpose resides in the heart—
beating in spirals within.

The moon is but a shadow-crescent,
though she'll soon return to light.
Circling, cycling, tenderly whispering:

Love is the hoop
where our truest truth resides.

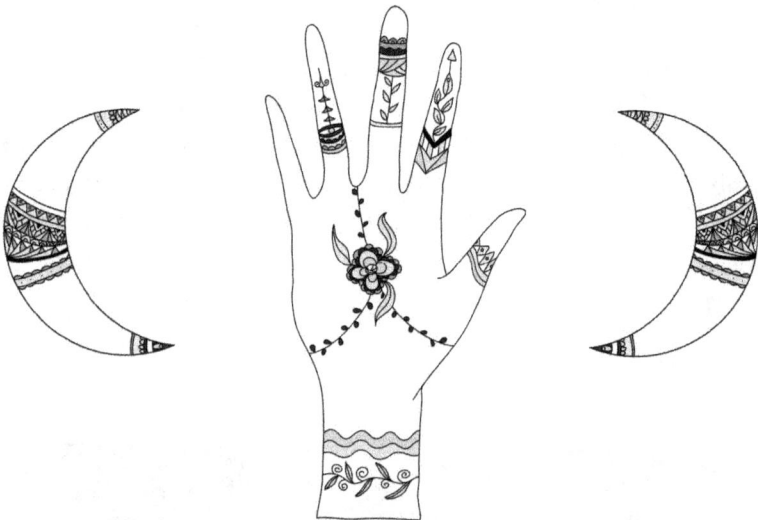

Shape Shifters

"It's no use going back to yesterday,
because I was a different person then."
—Lewis Carroll, *Alice in Wonderland*

We are not here to stay the same. People change and shapes shift. We have many moving parts and revolving roles. We can be 100 people in the span of a day or feel stagnant and stuck for what feels like months on end, only to surprise ourselves by springing into action like a supernova on fire.

Humans are fluid and so are feelings, subject to dynamic change. So are the muted-rainbow seasons and the soft-sorbet sky and the rise and set of the sun's tiger-eye. Even Mother Earth tilts and shifts her shape before our sight. While the universe keeps time in a dance of gold-magic and silver-star becoming.

Because all of us (each atom and cell and speck—that make up the endless doorways of this place) are dancing in time to the universe's lead and becoming who and what we are meant to be.

Shedding our tawny leaves when our season has turned. Phasing like pearl moon in its infinite cycles. We turn our face to the light and then to the dark. We descend and then ascend. *We are many and one, separate yet connected.* We find the light that has always been tucked in the core of our heart's grace-space. We realize ourselves forever changing, moving towards wholeness in our own different ways.

TIME TRAVELERS

If you turn the universe
on its side,
there you'll find doors
to a billion places.

Time bends,
space shakes,
stars collide—
we feel their dust collect
on the gaze of our faces.

Each of us is
a keeper of magic—
holding a world of wonder
all our own.

Our universe is only as big,
as our minds and hearts allow:
*The bigger you love
the further you'll roam.*

Traveling, raveling,
rippling, tripping,
stretching, reaching,
seeking, seeing—

*Forever returning to the soul
of our home.*

UPSIDE DOWN

Being human can be a very disorganized and disorienting experience. We can get lost in our own selves; truth is often found in those spaces. Sometimes we fall too deep in the mud and need somebody to help pull us out; truth is found in those spaces as well.

Hard things happen and we learn. Beautiful things happen and learning occurs there too. A tree can teach you how to stay grounded; a star how to shine; a drop of water how to still. We are given many teachers in our lifetimes, with our experience of self the biggest teacher of all.

Everybody's got problems rattling around in their minds, hearts, and bones—beneath the surface things can be a messy collection. The journey of the soul is to heal and to grow, it's certainly not about perfection.

I see you: wherever you find yourself today. I believe you: whatever truths you have to bear. I honor you: you are marvelously brave for being here my friend. I am with you: in this oneness of the journey we all share.

Let's help turn each other's flaws upside down, so we look at them differently, see the light shining through instead of the crack. Love is the key when we feel lost. Love is the key when we feel lack. *Love is the key: The compass that sits in the point of our hearts, eternally guiding us back.*

The Contrarian

Sometimes life will
teach it to us upside down:
from butterfly to cocoon
from tomb to womb.

Nautilus unspiraling.
Westward sunrise rising.
Clockwise counter timing.
Walking backward in a room.

Where Jupiter's retrograde
becomes heart's renegade
to learn new truths in contrary ways—
composing a symphony off-tune

(to break us down
and wake us out
and shake our former views)

My heart unloves
in beats and shades
becoming brighter with each moon:

To relearn love in greater ways—
loving backward in the room.

The Miracle of Breath and the Miracle of Death

Those who have passed before us would have us know that while we've got the miracle of breath part down—the felicitations, excitement, and sense of wonder that comes when a baby enters this world—we usually get the part about leaving it all wrong.

Death is a miracle. A rebirth and return to the light. It is a homecoming and a welcoming and a graduation rolled into one. Those who cross over greeted by those already waiting for them on the other side, who've seen and rejoice in the work that soul did in their time. Soul work we can't always grasp from the humanness of our eyes.

I see my brother sometimes in these casual moments and glimpses. He floats in a sea of ecstasy. Starlight and stardust; love-filled and light-bound. Everything magical that makes any of us tip our chins up to the moon on a full lit night and feel connected in a sense of awe, wonder, and vastness over the endless mysteries binding this universe.

We become bigger than ourselves in those moments. Bigger than the shells we call bodies that house who we know ourselves to be in this life. Bigger than the components that make up our days. Bigger than the satellites we call home and choose to return to night after night.

It's almost like we sense—in the infinite perplexity of the moment—how grand is the design and what a gift if it to have a place in that grandness, as the universe winks back and bids us remember our true selves.

You see, those who've passed know what so many of us have forgotten: We came from love, have always been connected to love, can never be separated from love, and we will return to the Source that is Love.

And so, though our human heart may break, our divine heart can know it is a miracle when they pass. A culmination, a beginning, a continuance, and an inception. The miracle does not stop, because a person leaves this place we call earth and their time here is at an end.

No, when you see it through the eyes of those who've gone before, the miracle of death is simply the moment when the free soul's birth springs forth

NEW EARTH

Sometimes the noise is so much that it makes me want to whisper. Go within and listen to soul's sounds, which tell me to find light in the fissures.

The hidden gems tucked in the cracks which others fail to quietly consider. There's a world of peace within these lines. Resilience and awareness lay. A multiverse of magic when you notice and remember—

Love is the language tucked in the seams, of all life's connection and in-betweens, weaving us closer in a web of dreams, where holiness transcends beliefs. There we'll find the place where we'll step into grace and bring ourselves back to the divine space of seeing the whole of our beauty.

Rain will be our symphony. Peace our ideology. Leadership a rainbow of wisdom and diversity. Trees will be our harmony. With mountains of serenity. All life will join hands in ushering equality. We'll transcend division's sin of fearing life's counter ecology. With empathy the narrative of humanity's anthology.

We'll change history's cosmology, as we create a new earth out of charity, hope and love.

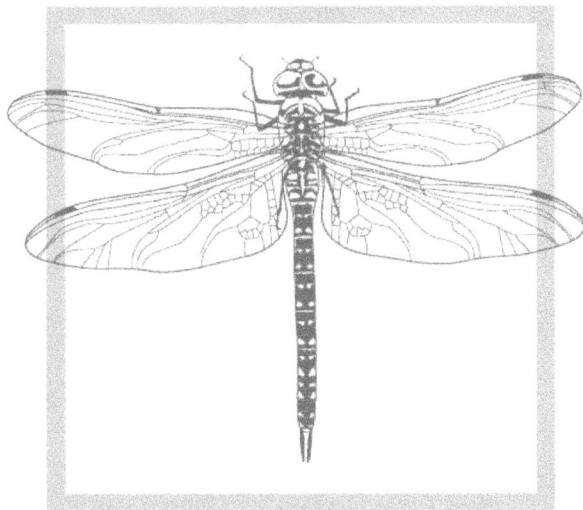

THE TRUTH WITHIN

You have to be prepared to take it.
To step into it.
To stand strong in it:
Your Space.

It is an acreage of being
nobody can claim but you,
a landscape of soul
only you can traverse.

Nobody else can know
the secrets of your heart,
my dear one.

Nobody can tell you who
you are or why you're here
or what purpose beats
when you press your
hand to the temple
in your chest
and *listen.*

Do you feel the warmth
residing there?
Do you sense the light
trying to shine through?
Do you hear the answer
to the question
of yourself:

You are made to be loved.
You are here for love.
You hold a universe
of love.

And that universe starts within you.

SOUL-COLLECTING

Always a work in progress.
Always in a state of becoming.
We ebb and flow and grow;
then ebb, flow, grow some more.

Finding our pieces along the way,
and bringing them back into ourselves,
so, we can crystallize, actualize and grow
new blooms in the garden of our full.

Like the trees, and the seas,
and the comings and goings of the breeze;
we keep soul-selecting and soul-collecting,
as we move towards our whole.

To Learn Self-Trust

Why is it so difficult to trust our experience of self when that same experience is often the key that holds the answer to our questions?

Why is it so difficult to trust our experience of self when our soul feels wrong and our core feels cold and our heart feels stuck, yet the world says this is the path we "should" take, so we keep on walking it instead of finding what we need to heed our own voice?

Why is it so difficult to trust our experience of self when there is nobody else capable of telling us about that experience except—our self?

What if we lived in such a way that we became our own experts. What if we treated our matter of soul as if there were no greater matter. What if we realized to love is to know the divine, and in so doing found the divine within ourselves.

How would things look different?

Where would we allow ourselves space to grow?

And most of all, if we embraced that deep, felt sense of innate soul trust—

Who might we become?

you
Are
gALaxies
Of Light

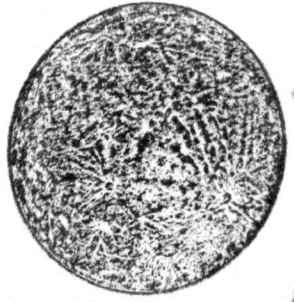

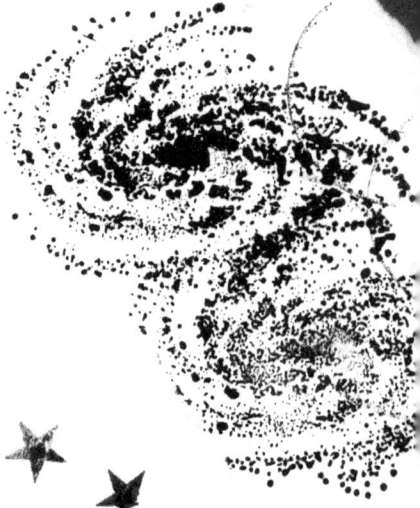

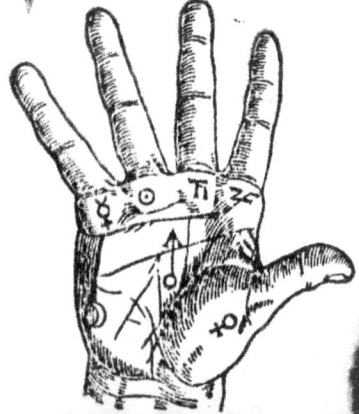

Algorithms, Astrology & Alchemy

things of sky, night, ideas and intuition

"DON'T TRY TO COMPREHEND WITH
YOUR MIND.
YOUR MINDS ARE VERY LIMITED.
USE YOUR INTUITION."

MADELEINE L'ENGLE, A WIND IN THE DOOR

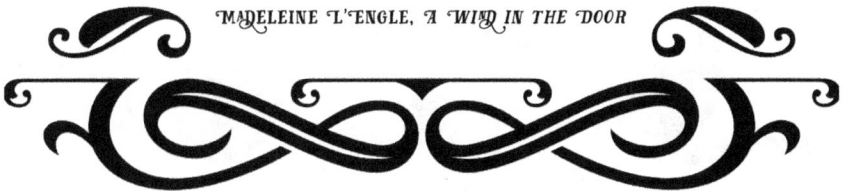

MOON CHILD

not quite of the land
nor quite of the sea
I make my home
somewhere in between—

like the citron crab
I travel in seams;
moon child's star
who seeks the unseen

in sand-scapes
and gnome-scapes
and forests of green. . .
I like to find emeralds
in pockets of gleam

where the light
hits just right
through my halcyon scenes

. . .filled with
visions of magic
and shamrock's fay dreams.

MYSTIC RIVER

Let life's bend
surprise you,
learn to lean into
its stead.

Dance with the cosmos
in untamed beat;
allow the unknown
to guide your thread.

Create your dreams
with starseed's soft weaves;
and dare to drift
where the angels do tread.
Through the eye
of mind's bright,
into visions of light,
where Merkabah's of love
do spread—

*(can you feel light's wings,
can you hear star's rings,
can you see moon's rings,
can you taste sky's springs?)*

Let the mystic river
ride you—
and choose to flow
where you're led.

CRESCENT

In my mind, I lay in her curve
a silvery, wintery slip of light
glimmering welcome and respite.

Up here, the world quiets below
myriads of lights, shimmering low
billions of hearts, same breath of sentience.

Starlight blinks and galaxies wink
tourmaline gleams among rubellite dreams
moon flickers nigh, luminescent—

And I in my mind, rest in her crescent.

SOLSTICE EVE

Solstice Eve is a time
for going under.

Soft shifts in light,
call me towards the sunset,
and dip me in star's wonder.

Nature speaks truth
in her endless transitions.
The moon cycles of our heart,
know how to listen
and heed her wisdom.

We contract and
then expand,
then slowly fade from dark to light
(there's revelation in-between,
bringing the invisible to sight).

Seeking, reaching,
believing and dreaming—
we embrace the face of change
and gentle winter's longest night.

From our darkest mood to our brightest light, we must learn to become like the moon and embody all parts of ourselves, seeing the sacred in all. Always changing, always shifting, yet completely at peace with our faces and phases — knowing each aspect of being provides a valuable contribution to the cycle of our whole.

Hanalei Night

cerulean blue
sea-salt sweeps;
evening comes
with apricot light

soft pink thinks
& mermaids drink;
water chases
emerald tide

red boat sails

with whispered tales;

so many mysteries

of celestite flight

and here I sit
'neath sunset's spell;
as day slips
into Hanalei night

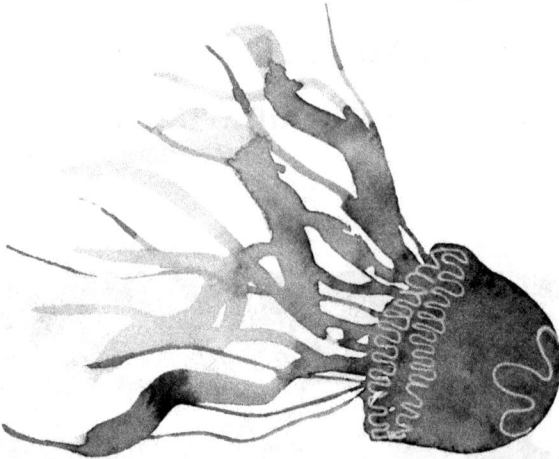

Idea Finders

Get out of the box: be an experience collector, an idea finder, a gatherer of being and noticing. *Talk to the trees and learn the beauty of seeing and listening.*

Pay attention to the perspective shifts that come from bell curve's interruptions and life's seeming disruptions: sometimes disruptions are truth's eruptions, necessary to rearrange and realign earth's soul. Learn to be fluid and accept life's invitation to shift and flow. Show up for yourself in as many ways as you can, and in so doing you will find you are showing up for the whole.

Let all that doesn't grow you fall away, so you keep finding brave ways to grow. Be relentless in pursuing your right to delight. Breathe deeply. Walk authentically. Let your heart be your guide and your sight.

Radiant Sky Woman

She came from the sky.
Radiant streams of light,
fingertips graced with
fire,
wonder,
perseverance,
and blindsight.

Forgetting who she was,
leaving behind her memories,
taking this form
to live the life
her soul's commitment
agreed to be.

She always found herself
wandering up high,
trying to touch the night;
she sensed the stars held
answers to
the nameless
why's she cried.

She spent three years
in solitude—
her heart the beat
of fortitude;
she learned the mystery
of this place
is only found
through breath and grace.

By the time
she knew her name,
she'd grown so much
her being changed,
broken,
reshaped,
rearranged—
her purpose clear,
her path displayed.

She went her own way
and if asked to explain—
she'd simply say:

I am here to teach others about Love.

A Case of the Mondays

Monday is the color
of fresh cream
and grasshopper green dreams,
which spring into fruition
from our tiny hops and springs.
Possibilities are clean at
the dawn of a new week;
fresh breath is gleaned
through aventurine seas
and Monday's moony beams.
The world sits waiting
ready to bless our needs,
asking us how we'll receive
its endless eggshell beauty?
Reminding us we only need
turn our face to the sun,
palms to sky…

Then breathe, relieve, conceive—
Believe.

SNOWFLAKES

Everybody has their own process, their own way of being in the world. Like snowflakes with individual patterns of sacred geometry, each of us forms differently, sterling ice crystals dancing through air taking a unique path to the ground.

People forget it's not easy being a snowflake.

They forget we are formed through cold, and ice, and dust; yet manage to create crystalline beauty on our fall to the earth. Anything sensitive enough to form in these conditions has an underlying strength that many may miss, if all they see is the seemingly fragile grace.

Because we often underestimate what looks soft and don't recognize it for what it is—a gift of beauty that only became beautiful by allowing life's alchemy to shape it. We miss the lion-strength found in vulnerability, emotions, creativity, heart knowledge, and love.

It is only in tapping into these sacred veins of receptivity that we can find our own unique path. Because the more we try and quiet our intuitions and sensitivities, the more we lose our shape and look like everybody else. And when we look like everybody else, we staunch our own call, which is trying to break through and speak truth—

Helping us return to the home of our soul, so we can better see our way and find the beauty of our own divine, crystalline flake.

SERPENTINE HYMNS

you go talk to the snow
and I'll go talk to
the wind:

I'll meet you between
in the kyanite sky
where the angelite doves
still swim...

in sodalite streams
on chrysoprase dreams
through the iolite waters
within...

we'll sail away
in our bottle of blue,
on the waves of
serpentine hymns.

INDIGO DREAMS

can visions birth inside of us
without us knowing
where or why or how;
creativity's compulsion calls
a universe born in a blink
starlight winks
in cusps of crimson curls.
nectarine dreams surround
the nape of nocturnal night—
within each sleep,
a world completes
and we wake on the crest
of inception's indigo eyes.

We will always be together
and never die

New Moon in Aries

New moon sits
black
a raven hovering over
a silent silk sea,
face turned inwards
in serenity and wanting
she returns to herself,
to the darkness within,
consumed by
shadows wane calling.

We think the way
to the stars is up,
but really it is down
in the mud:
when one learns to dig
so deep in their core
they break through
to the other side—
emerging from nebula's night.

Finding new sky on
the hem of horizon
and diamonds in
their seams of light.

SHADOWLANDS

O ur shadows are as important as our light. They are the space where we find our hidden depths and the irritant grains of sand where our pearls are formed. Anytime I've been through a dark period, a depression, a grief journey: *I always come out the other side and realize I've collected gifts along the way—even if I couldn't see them at the time.*

It's hard to give ourselves permission to be in a dark space. It's uncomfortable. Often, it's very painful. Heartache, sorrow, and difficult feelings are stormy seas to sail, and we will crave fairer waters and the grace of sunlight. We crave feeling good. We sometimes judge and blame ourselves for not being able to pull out of it. Or we wonder what is wrong with us, because we think we *should* feel better.

But there is nothing wrong with us. The shadow self is a part of who we are and learning to work through our own darkness is part of being whole and being human. Often the tools that help lift us up on a 'normal bad day' fail us in the shadows. There's just not enough substance, grit, or real to those tools.

Yet substantive, authentic living is both real and gritty. Which means we are going to get dirty from time to time.

So, sometimes we have to allow the dirt. Try and navigate dark terrain the best we know how, and make peace with the fact that we feel a lot of things that aren't often peaceful. *Know that unpeaceable emotions are part of the full spectrum of being human.* Great creativity can come from conflict and chaos.

There are gifts in dissolution. Shadows are where we find evolution. Being in a dark place doesn't mean we're not transforming, or shining our soul light, or of less value or worth. It doesn't mean we've lost our way. *It simply means we're busy being a human being who is engaged in the process of allowing for our full scope.*

STORM'S EYE

*A storm will teach you
many things.*

How thunder shakes fierce
and lightening's flash high;
reminding how little we are
in the scope of this life.

How to stay calm when everything
quivers; and how to unleash
our own power when
it's no longer time
for calm.

Somewhere in wind's silver eye
I can almost hear him speak:
*he gusts of truths of yesterday
and unveils ancient things.*

Small in his wake
all I can do is look in his face
and listen—

And realize, like he,
we're in constant motion,
and can be no other than
who, what and when
we're called to be.

Stars

"All men have stars, but they are not the same things for different people. For some, who are travelers, the stars are guides. For others they are no more than little lights in the sky. For others, who are scholars, they are problems... But all these stars are silent. You—You alone will have stars as no one else has them."
—Antoine de Saint-Exupéry, *The Little Prince*

The stars hold millions of secrets and mysteries. Beacons of light here to guide and inspire; they shine down—a world of their own—bringing hope to our world.

Ancient way showers, scattered eons ago put in place long before us, they have piloted, inspired, comforted, and awed for century upon century of millennia. We come into this world at a particular point in time, and in so doing choose a celestial star map, by which we can guide

Galactic magic makers, stars make us believe anything is possible they give us hope and bring us a sense of shelter in the storm, calm in cacophony, and finding the light when all else seems black. It is impossible to look at the stars and not to dream, hope and wish

Stars are the gateway that lead us up into the cosmos, expanding our wonder of the divine. One step closer to heaven, they help us think upwards and expand in kind. Here to remind us how small we are and how infinite it is out there:

We shine down so you have hope, we shine down so you can see. We twinkle to remind you to lighten up. We hold a dance of particles inside of ourselves, a miracle of motion, reminding that you too hold the same ecstatic dance inside of you.

Remember—just as we stare up at the stars in splendor and amaze they are staring down in wonder and grace, thinking how brave it is for us to be human in this place.

MINTANKA

She remembered the place, with endless spans of glassy seas. Where peace reigned supreme, and the priestess unleashed the sacred winds. Who rang ancient hymns, waking the light we carry within.

There may always be a part of her who yearns for that space—where the clear waters grace in crystal clarity for miles. And the suns are so bright, even in the dark one can always find and guide by the light.

Her wandering soles keep searching for home and her place in the whole of this world's pattern and soul. Restless feet made replete, as she wanders in longing. Baby bird, trying to find her true nest and return to her place of belonging.

Then a breeze comes in through forest's glen, and the sky says: *Hush now, hush even Star Travelers need rest and time to heed their heart's singings and songings.*

She looked at the sky towards Orion's belt, now a delta in space where her home once dwelt. Only accessed with memory and the visions she felt. Her heart a pool of turquoise melt. Now she carried her home inside her self—

Listening to the ancient winds of need, following the unseen star-road of belief, as her soles returned to Love.

QUIET SPACES

Everybody needs solitude.
Quiet spaces to curl into and sink.
Think. Delve. Seek.
Be in the stillness on the cusp of retreat.
Burrow into the recesses of mind, heart, and dream.
Breakthroughs come from turning inwards; epiphanies arise when we
pause for release.
A full moon is rising, new truths are revealing.
The path to heart's matter is found through silent peace.

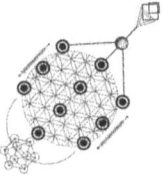

Galactic Symphony

They come to me
in wake-sleep,
appearing
in my dream-speak:
cosmic messengers
of celestial mirth
who help us delve
the rhythms unseen.

Neptune plays
a trident symphony
of intuition, illusion
and mystic mystery.

Jupiter teaches
expansion and reach,
a scholar of wisdom
who grows the
mind's beliefs.

Uranus
the rebel child
helps us keep
our inner wild.

Pluto evolves
transforms and renews,
while Moon makes us feel
all those watery blues.

Saturn constricts
and often restricts,
but if you stick with her list
you'll master your grist.

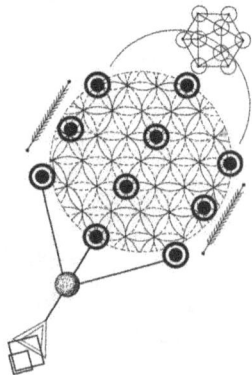

Chiron wounded healer tries
to heal the wound
that pierced our side,
so we transcend the pain
and find the light.

Mars says: *stand tall*
and let your fiery
self achieve.

While Venus brings
beauty, love, relationship,
and artistry.

And Mercury, in its
thoughtful circuitry,
bids us to say what
we think and to think
what we mean.

Sun at the center
who draws us towards light,
helping us each, in our
own way, shine bright:

A galactic coalition,
of astrological distribution,
giving us clues to our unique composition—
when we pause to turn nigh.'

Let star's intuition guide,
hear constellation's cry
turn our faces up high—
and seek towards the sky.

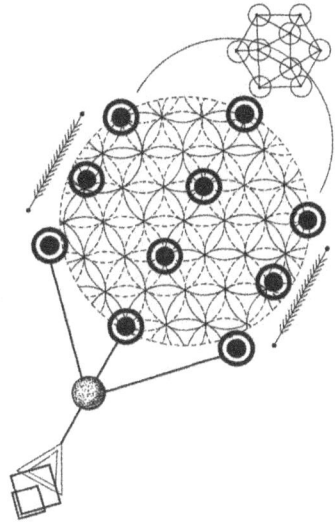

Horizons Unseen

Take unknown paths and look for new delights with adventure and curiosity. Recognize that every time you choose the unknown over the familiar, you are entering into a deeper relationship of trust with universe's intelligence and life's creative mysteries.

Believe you will be supported, and you will. Know you will be guided, and it shall be so.

Fly far from anything that seeks to bind you to the gravity of certainty, and with faith and fortitude as your forceful wings glide towards the skies of horizons unseen. Through star-bright and heart-light and soul-shine and moon-dreams, become the cartographer of your uncharted seas.

Intuition's Speak

Intuition is an invisible force of wisdom and knowledge, which exists inside each and every one of us.

We can't see it. We can't measure it. We can't tangibly manifest it or take it out for show and tell—and yet it is a real, divine, inner compass that guides us and helps us follow our heart path. And this invisible, but extremely potent energy, is the same energy which helps us perceive and understand the world around us with deeper meaning, tiers, and dimensions.

Coincidence, synchronicity, and gut feelings take on deep meaning to those working with their intuition. All of this is accessed through honing our natural intuitive abilities, so we become heart-seers, who know how to receive and see, and wisdom-keepers, who know how to discern and inform.

Our intuition connects us to the universe inside of ourselves and the multitude of worlds that exist in our chambers of self. It also connects us to the universe outside of us—which we are very much a participant in—and allows us to access wisdom from the collective conscious, the collective unconscious, and the spiritual realms.

One of the beautiful things about working with our intuition and learning to receive messages from the universe is learning our own language of soul. *This is the holy mystery. The alchemy of spirit, which can only be understood through the heart and a vivid, juicy, quantum relationship with life's cues and clues.*

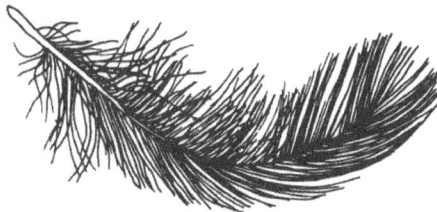

GHOST DANCERS

Evening sinks us into softer spaces.
Day's edge blurs, while moon's dissolution makes all shades melt together in fluid amalgamation. Everything flows with harmonic phases.

Grief becomes love, and sad becomes tender, and despair becomes hope, as our hearts become ghost dancers honoring the sacred of all of life's schisms. Crickets chirp and frogs whir and somewhere in jungle's stir—ancient drums begin to play thrumming and pulsing in sacred grove rhythms.

They are light songs of deepest truth, if you learn to listen.

Spelled out through star's ink, scrawled in the stems of the clean evergreens, sustained by the growth of the banyan trees. Singing, seeking, embracing, and teaching; sweet music that hearkens we embrace our own living.

Reminding us the miracle is breathing and being.

The moon hides her face as she travels to void, yet soul casts light when vision wanes. The ancestor's watch as the cycle turns night, the ghosts they dance in endless pace. Spectrals of peace who honor what's passed, keeping time with the beat of the magic and grace.

Everything fades in eve's soft in-between, until nothing is left 'cept for love's endless face.

ECLIPSE

we are not brought
into the darkness to stay
in the darkness, but only for a time
until we journey towards new light

no moon phase lasts forever
*(each shade of truth
is what makes us whole)*
new to half, return to bright

and I promise you this shall pass:
for faith is keeping vision
in the absence
of sight

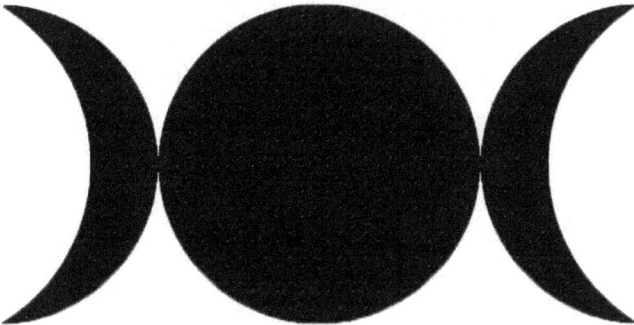

DEVELOP A GAZE OF CURIOSITY, WHICH
HELPS YOU DIG BENEATH THE SURFACE
AND SEE THE STRANGE BEAUTY IN THIS
JOURNEY OF BEING HUMAN.

SUNDAY LOVE SONGS

They did astrology
on a Sunday and talked
of matters in the stars
over bottles of pink tea
and queries of Libra in rising.

While Bobby kept on singing
love songs about rain and how
loving her was never
gonna change.

It was the kind of day
that makes one want to stay at home,
tucked into heart's way—
Listening to the rhythmic drops
over love and tea and rain.

SKY RHYMES

Half-moon tilts
in silver chalcedony;
new day breathes
on iolite's breeze.

Somewhere beneath,
earth's heart sings—
through pewter blues
and aquamarine wings.

Silvery grays dance
with agate lace wisps;
amethyst's soft 'gainst
the nape of snow's kiss.

The sky collides
in symphonic rise—
a crystalline grid
composed of rhymes,
for those who see
with lucent eyes
and seek the mysteries
between the lines.

*Underneath
the selenite bright,
my mind stills for love.*

HOPE ON HORIZON

My dear one—
I know this time
has been a sting
of haze and pain
and in between.

That your bones
hold secrets
few know,
your heart an untold
tale of silence.

And yet, the
glistening winds sweep,
the shifting clouds speak,
and there is hope
on the new moon
of horizon.

Love is tucked
in corners unseen,
grace notes play
on autumn's gold leaves,
your soul holds
a blazing, starlit fire
no eyes can see—

And my dear one,
I believe in You.

Manifesto of Hope

I believe in people and their ability to change themselves. I truly do. I see our minds and hearts and bodies and ability to reason, feel love, breathe, and engage with the world around us as the biggest game changers there will ever be.

I believe when we need support and community it's important to seek out spaces we feel supported and connected. But I also believe, at the end of the day, people are their own experts and wisdom keepers and harbingers of love. The right support can help hold up a mirror to reflect those gifts to us, but they can't do the work for us.

At the end of the day, you are what YOU have, which means your own experience of self is going to be the most valid. If thought patterns and belief systems, and ways of being are not resonating for you and with you, then I believe in changing them.

Like Walt Whitman said: Dismiss anything that insults your soul.

We learn so much through trial and error. What worked for us at one point in time may not at another, as we are continually breathing evolving, and being. That's why life can often be so messy. There's a lot of experimentation going on throughout the whole thing. Most 'experts' may have a lot of wisdom, but they don't have your answers— only you do.

So, keep being present with yourself. Keep listening to you. Reevaluate thoughts and internal constructs—*especially when they aren't working for you.* Be an architect of thoughts who roots your ideology in radical self-love.

Draw close to people and ideas and perspectives, which support you and encourage your process. Release all else that wasn't meant for you. Drop into your heart, body, and intuitive wisdom. Breathe into the winds of your own change. *Keep going about the work of constructing a life in this world (from the inside out), which supports the whole of you.*

OBSIDIAN LIGHT

New moon, purple rain falls
cool lavender streams
greet ink's midnight

A gentle ballad, water and wine
turning darkness into
obsidian light

The grass inhales then exhales
*(I wonder if others can
feel-see the earth breathe?)*

Slowly we curl on the wings
of the moon, she and me
one in the mysteries

She speaks on the voice of
an amethyst dream:

Let Love Lead. Let Love Lead. Let Love Lead.

Starseed

*Free your need
dear starseed—*

Don't you know
it's time to
shake up,
shake in,
shake out,
break out—
and let the world
know your shine?

Shrinking and
blinking your light
away, won't serve
anyone in this
time.

*Wield that love
dear starseed—*

You've stayed in
the shadows
past nigh'
waking
then quaking
and soul liberating—
releasing your fear
that your big
is too wide,
because it is now time
for your BIG
to arrive.

Own your call
dear starseed—

The one who
helped open
mind's eye:

You've questioned
yourself for
far too long
and now you must
own your wise.

Live your truth
dear starseed—

You're supported by
light of your tribe,
you're here for
a reason,
your dark
had a season,
but now it's your
time to arise:

So free yourself
dear starseed,
and let that
soul-light
shine.

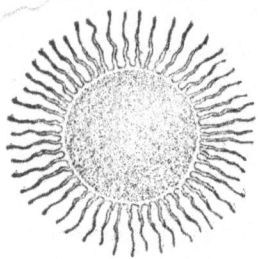

everyOne
shines
in
tHeir
Own tiMe

22 2

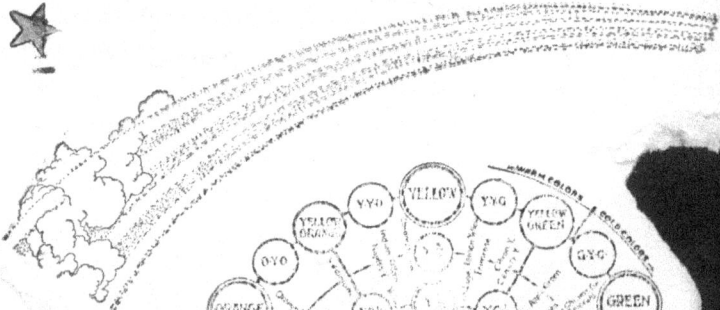

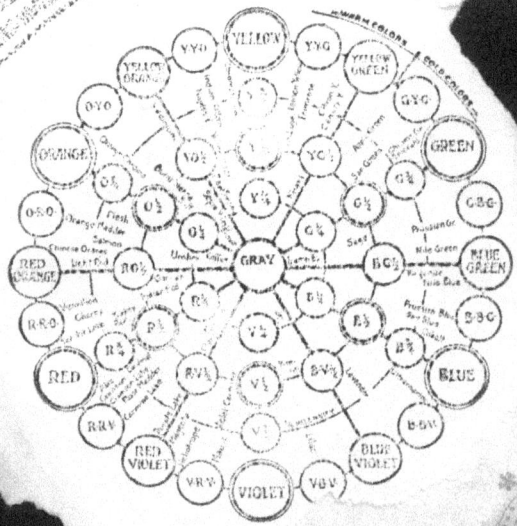

Magic, Muse

&

Mystery

things of light, love, divinity and creativity

"HAPPINESS CAN BE FOUND,
EVEN IN THE DARKEST OF
TIMES, IF ONE ONLY REMEMBERS
TO TURN ON THE LIGHT."

J. K. ROWLING, *HARRY POTTER*

Sunshine Makers

Make your own sunshine.
Notice the joy.
Find the light gleaming
between the cracks.

Let grace craft your day.
Allow and receive.
Keep choosing
prosperity over lack.

Have faith in your process.
Witness your gifts.
Let love be the light,
which fills your heart-pack.

Believe you are worthy.
Keep pressing forth.
Lift your face to the sky
and don't look back.

QUANTUM HEART: To love so radically you bring love into all spaces inside of yourself—your dark, your deep, your pains, your breaks—until you discover there is no part of yourself that is unlovable, and through learning to love your own multi-dimensions, your heart, in turn, becomes quantum- dimensional and able to hold more space for love.

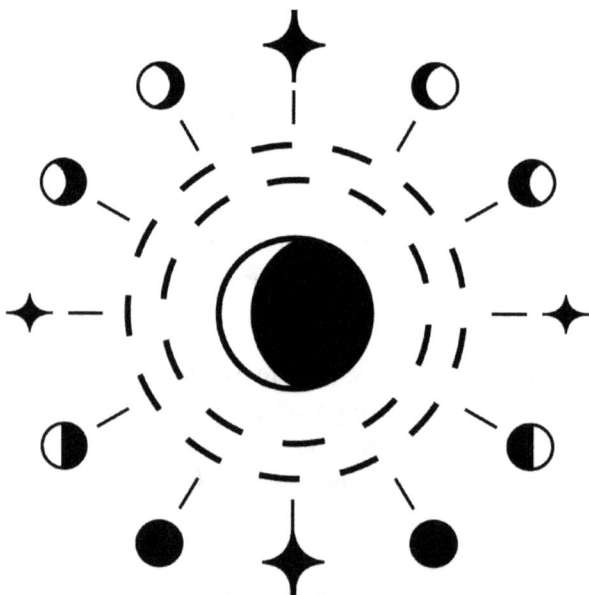

Agape

Love cannot be
captured or kept—
it is a free agent,
available to all
who choose its path.

Never wanting.
Never lacking.
Never elusive—
always there for those
who choose to allow
it in their hearts.

An attestation
of light's affirmation
that simply imparts:

Yes. It's true. Love lives here.

magick

MOSAICS

how and who
we become
is not always up
for us to decide—
as if we could predict
the unpredictable
nature of life
that shapes
and breaks
and makes us
pieced and whole

riotous collage,
finely crafted porcelain,
textured mosaic,
brightly tiled backsplash;
a constant composition
—*we are works of*
walking art—
and we each
come together
in our own ways

forever changing
forever rearranging
forever finding truth
among
the patterns
in our shades

WINGS

In my art I am free
to be a littler me,
who knows to be *Big*
is to smile and to dream

of magical places
and unicorn gazes
and sugar pink glazes
that frost cupcake's faces.

In my art I am free
to go far beyond me,
travel new worlds
where the stars swim the seas

where the sky's always pink
lit with crystalline rings,
where rainbows sing soul-sounds
and color's supreme.

In my art I am free
to be all shades of me,
there's no holding back
creativity's wings

who fly with the fairies
and swim whale songs deep,
who soar Serengeti
and see sacred things.

These wings are my gateway
to halcyon dreams,
*where peace reigns eternal
and love is the king.*

BIRDS

131 ways to sing joy
or maybe there's more

i started losing track
after counting to 100,
so thick on
the branch
they sit

chimeral chirps
riotous melody
oh to be so free,
and noise so blissfully

harmony
peace
migration
liberty—

these are the things
of which they sing,
these are the songs
i remember my wings . . .

    fly

        fly

            fly

up to the blue
beyond the green

Juicy-Fruit Truth

F ind the sunshine in the day's sweet swing. Look for the good then take the time to notice its zing. Do something that makes you feel about five, then do something that makes you feel wise; know these can be the very same thing.

Create music in your heart. See your day as joyful art. *Throw imaginary cherry tarts up in the sky-pie-high and fly on the wings of the script that's your part.*

Because only you can play the role of YOU and embody your being with juicy-fruit truth. You see, the universe cast you carefully as the soul that you are. So, make the most of your day, embrace what beauty you may, and see the gleaming—bling of your glorious star.

CHANGE, PEACE & ART

Show up where you feel called to show up. Look for ways to bring more love into the world. Remember that it begins inside your own heart and energy field.

Feel all that you need to feel about what you need to feel, transmute those feelings into change, peace, and art.

More head pats and belly laughs. Less dreaming short and playing small. *This is your life—grab onto it and bring in all the love you can.*

GRACE REBELS

It takes a lot of courage to work on bringing a more radical sense of acceptance towards yourself. It takes a lot of courage to drop into your own being and learn to sit within that space. It takes a lot of courage to see the transcendent lovely in the strain of human hard.

In other words, it takes a lot of courage to be a grace rebel. It is a sacred act of rebellion when we choose to bring love into spaces that feel unlovable. It is a sacred act of rebellion to see the holy in the dark.

It is a sacred act of rebellion when we choose to fully acknowledge and make space for our hurt, pain, anger, bitterness, hate, resentment, and sorrow. Because every shadow aspect is a creature in disguise: tricksters who teach us about the darkest, hardest stuff inside of ourselves, so we can learn about humanity and compassion, and actively choose love.

So, we can be a grace rebel who answers grace's invitation with a 'yes,' inviting it into all spaces inside of ourselves, realizing they are all worthy of love.

Realizing our process is just that: a process. It's not something right or wrong, good or bad, better or worse—it is simply the evolution of our own eco-system of being.

Capable Heart

You're going
to have to learn
to be strong
dear one.

Not strong in
the way where
you hold it all
together;
strong in the
way where you
find the courage
to *break*
and let life
have its way
with your capable
heart—

Who has so
much more to give
than she's been
given space for.

Some nights
are going to
feel dark;
days may feel
long;
but each step
away is a step
towards
the freedom to
rediscover the
places you
belong.

So, breathe deep
my friend,
and hold on—
this end will be
your start;
to help you grow
beyond this place—

*And live the truth
of your capable
heart.*

Hope's Hum

I like to tilt my gaze towards the sunlight as often as I can. Sometimes it's not always easy, but I've learned the sun is always shining, even when we can't see it through the clouds. And that belief is where hope intersects in my life, playing a steady hum of beauty, prosperity, and faith in the unseen.

What brings you hope?

Whatever it is, wrap it in blankets to keep it safe and warm—even as you release it on feathered wings to fly to sky and grow your dream. Let hope sing and help you march to the beat of your own probability. Strum your banjo of sunshine and opportunity; believe in your seeds of self and sow them far and freely.

Know—and it shall be so—you're moving in the direction of your highest possibility.

JAR

If you can find a way
to unscrew the cap
from the jar of life,
and dive into its
firefly mess:
you'll find light in
unnoticed places,
and breath in the
whirl of the press.

You'll notice magic awaits
in hematite visions,
malachite grace,
and dragon-eye dreams—

And even in the gasps
of grief's gray grit,
you will find your way through
if you hold on to belief:

Love is the key
to the doorway of soul
a gateway that takes us
to soul-scapes of whole,
which helps us remember
our truth of the stars—

And find our way back,
through the earth of the jar.

PHOENIX

birds
and chimes
and everything green
on the cusp of
almost too hot,
but still tolerable
—Phoenix in
the spring

within the heat
and city streets,
I sit under familiar trees
—in a residence
of busyness
and people jams
and city blooms—
their shady leaves
spread wide
reach high
offering cool
sanctuary

painted skies
they call to me
fluorescent pink,
soft lavender,
muggy blue
and sweeps of breeze,
sweep the heat
   away
     up
       off
sonoran's saffron
chimneys

a tiny square of
yards and dogs
and friendship
old and true,
each time I'm here
I find relief

each time I come
—to the valley of sun—
I leave with
something
golden,
warm,
renewed

A BILLION LOVES

My dear one,
don't let them
get you down,
or tell you who
to be,
when you are
a burnished light
designed
to shine bright,
and not be
diminished
by eyes with
clouded sight.

Not everybody
can stand to see
the moon on
fire or the sun
in her glorious
mantle of white.

So, chin up,
heart open,
feet grounded,
and eyes wise;
for my dear one
you are a universe of a billion loves,
whose face lights up
the night.

The crux of living soulfully and creatively is to just keep owning your ability to be an innovative greatrix with whatever ingredients you are given.

IGNITION

F an passion's flames. Allow the stillness of your mind to inspire the burn of deep inner knowing. See each step as movement towards. Believing you are building the life of your dreams *(even if you're not sure what you are growing)*.

Allow the universe to conspire in your fire and help plant seedlings in your core-light and emotional-mire. So, you find your diamonds in this world's mud—and toss them up to the stars with wild desire.

Believe you can, and you shall. Know it will be okay and it will. See yourself as an inspired being to admire: a unique blueprint of stars circling zodiacs of endless spire.

Embrace your constellations in the light of the coals. Choose to see yourself as spirit-kissed, lion-brave and utterly whole. *Fan passion's flames with muse's bonfire and ignite the eternal fire of your soul.*

Love is a Holy Circle

Do tiny things of care. Even small acts have ripple effects, and we never know who we'll touch with our intentional deeds of compassion.

Find a higher and wiser perspective: use this as your touchstone every time your personal perspectives are challenged. Let the two chisel away at one another, as you become wiser in the process and your higher perspective stretches and grows through trial and truth.

Be an activist for grace. Be an activist for kindness. Be an activist for love. Stand up for what you believe in, but work on refusing to feed the agenda of smugness, strife, and hate. Set good boundaries around those who do feed that agenda. Take things back into yourself when you begin to lose yourself; find your silence; drop into your truth; *listen.* Be slow to react and quick to consider.

A thoughtful pause can make all the difference between creative construction or divisive destruction.

Do the repair work when you realize you got it wrong; remember this repair work begins within. Build so many bridges inside of yourself that you are filled with rainbows of peace, then take that empathic connection out into the rest of the world and build more rainbows. Know that, *I don't know, I'm still figuring it out,* is a perfectly acceptable response.

Give yourself space to wrestle with uncertainty: your future self will thank you for allowing them room to grow. If you don't like something change it, and if you can't change it, then keep on changing you so you don't become like it.

Know that most people are reacting out of a place of separation, hurt and pain. The path of peace doesn't mean you can't set healthy borders around yourself when you encounter these people, it just means your wiser self sees what's really going on in their soul. So you keep working to forgive and release, so as not to attach and become that pain yourself.

Remember, love is a holy circle: There are no sides. Love needs no sides. Love knows no sides. Love has no sides.

SOUL SPEAK

The world around us is speaking all the time. The trees sway and send calm resolution: Stand tall in your truth to find grounded solution.

Flowers burst with cheer and clear truth: *Bloom, be bigger be magnificently you.*

The hum of the fridge could be spirit's way of saying: *Stop freeze, and pay attention—something is trying to come through if you give it pause and listen.*

The brush of silk might flutter your fingers with wonder and remind: *Tread softly, go gently—your strength is in knowing when to let go, receive, and unwind.*

11:11's and 2:22's might speak truth to you, making you aware of the presence of angelic hues. Just as a 9 becomes a guidepost to return to inward soul, while a 3 may tell you conjunction's replete when we seek harmony with the whole.

Ever wonder why you feel bell's sound or taste earth's green or sense music's resonant speak? The universe is a chatterbox communicating through anything, if we can keep making space to learn, to notice, to hear, to love, to receive.

Everything can be a messenger when we begin to connect and see. Dream-weave and animal-speak and coinciding-synchronicity. The soft of pink, the power of red, the clarity of clear blue aquamarine.

Ocean's unending tides remind us to ride the flow of life. Wind's stir, moon's rise, and sun's shine dance the cycles of change and time.

The more we expand our relationship with the language of the soul: *The more the universe keeps coming alive and our consciousness grows. And in the rhythm of spirit's syntax, speech and beats, our hearts delve into the mysteries and find their deeper knows.*

Sundays are for Silence

I am learning in the golden hush of these October days that sometimes you must crawl back to yourself and *demand you sue for solitude.*

The nature of an introvert, intuitive, empath heart is a matter that can only be realized alone. The heart is the gateway to all that's divine; self-discovery the doorway to soul. We are not owed to each other, each soul path differs and sometimes the holiest of words is *No.*

Obligations can become cages. Resisting change a stalemate that keeps things the same. Boundaries are conventions we're meant to transcend, and honoring our experience of self is how we remember our way.

Autumn comes with guavas fall. Ripened saffron, blush nectar, ocean songs interlace. Tangled up in their path, I return to my self. Bended knee, heart in hand, listening to my forever always *(whatever you do, stay true to you)*—

Honoring the sacred silence of the gift of a Sunday.

The Equalizer

Love
makes no measure,
takes no measure,
gives no measure
of us all.
Equally
available from
the gutter to the temple:
it judges none,
its strings of grace
wrapped around
our hearts, our lives
our gains, our falls.
I used to wish
to be more than,
to be worthy,
to be loved—
Now I'm learning as I go
(even our dimmest dark)
grace is written
on our souls—

We have
never been apart from
the face of love's whole.

Untamed Art

Can you learn to sit
with the not knowing.
With your own
unanswered questions
of self whose answers
are met with more questions—
an unclear picture,
a half-finished puzzle,
whose pieces are still
being collected
as you go.

Can you learn to drop
into your own space
of nebula.
Learn to trust the process
for being what it is—
the unsolved mystery
of you, whose
resolution and absolution
can only be discovered
through your living.

Can you learn to love
the wild unknown—
that uncanny space
where the wild things
grow and dreams are
discovered and star-wishes
are met with magic dust,
preparing your path,
creating your next step:

Inviting you to be
an admirer of the beauty
of your own becoming,
and make peace with
the untamed art
that is you.

Rose Gardens

There's a lot of chatter and buzz in this world telling you who to be, and how to be, and that you have to do it a certain way.

The only way I know to keep living our authentic truth is to take things back to a space of ourselves. To engage in solitude so we can create space for our higher selves and higher truths to come in. To wade through the world's chatter—sifting the sands for any gems of wisdom which *do* serve.

And to always keep tapping into our own heart wisdom, which is endlessly available to guide and direct us.

Be intentional about creating space. Challenges external messages. Open your mind's eye and examine all things for truth. Place your hand on your heart often and ask yourself—*How do I feel about this and what do I need to know for my highest truth?*

Invite spirit into the mix and ask for deeper wisdom. Live life from the inside out. Create rose gardens in your heart. Plant seeds of authenticity in the entirety of your being. Water them with pause, and still, and soft and quiet. Allow yourself space to grow.

Place your hand on your heart in gratitude for all you're becoming and all you've become.

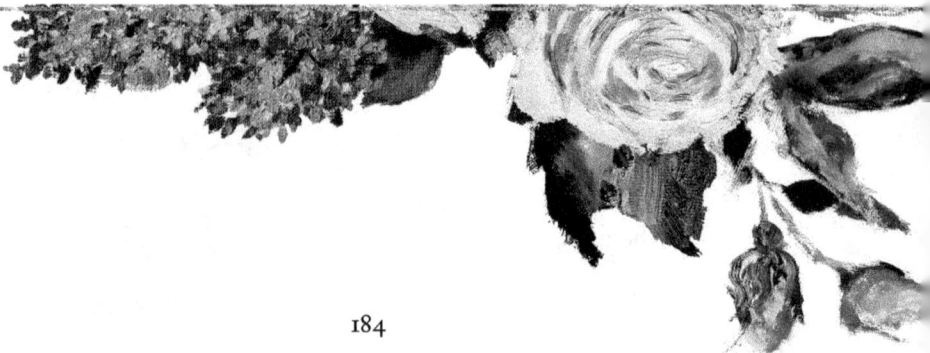

GOLD TIPPED LEAVES

You are not your thoughts,
your history, your feels or
the shell of your
outer identity.

But you are your heart,
your spirit, your soul,
and the universe of wisdom,
which lays in-between.

You are your joy
and delight and the moments
you collect like jewel-dipped,
gold-tipped leaves.

You are your ability
to stay open to love,
to be kind, and to drop
into life and receive.

You are sunshine
and starlight and
lavender moonbeams.
*So, take heart and listen
to the spirit-songs
of your soul-dreams.*

Let them lead, feed, and seed
your deepest desires
and needs.

And know you are a
nebula of unending light—
who flies with galaxies
of fathomless wings.

LION HEART

My dear lion heart,
don't you know—
it all unfolds
according to the
patterns of your soul.

In polka-dot waves
and plaid idiosyncrasies;
through signs and shades
and cosmic synchronicities;
your tesselate tapestry
weaving the way
to the intricate path
of your soul's galaxy.

My dear lion heart,
I know you think
you still have a
way to go:

But stop and find ease
for how far you've stepped,
and know your journey
is already whole.

Your magnitude
of exactitude
will tell you
don't rest when
the currents mid-flow.

But I say *pause*
and watch the clouds
shift. . .
then drift
lift & sift
'long the current's
blue tow.

My dear lion heart,
you'll sow
then you'll grow
and in the end, all leads
back to your soul.

Whose rhythms
and rhymes
and triangle beats,
chime with the time
of your wandering feet
—who walk in a line
of invisible belief—
following your shine
and letting heart lead.

So, don't be worried
you'll miss the boat,
or lose your way,
or that life will withhold
the future dreams
you'll embody and own:

Because don't you know,
my dear girl, it all unfolds
according to the patterns
of your soul.

LOVE IS A BLESSING AND A MYSTERY.
YOU DON'T REALLY KNOW WHAT'S GOING
TO HAPPEN WITH IT—
IT IS ITS OWN WILD FORCE
WHICH GROWS UNTAMED.

EARTH ANGELS

B e an earth angel for someone else. Take time to lift them up. Send a card, send light, make a call, spend time. Know that supporting others doesn't always require much effort and mire, just intention followed by action and sincere desire.

Be an earth angel for the planet. Love the earth. Treat her well. Talk to animals and learn the gifts of the plants. Offer tobacco in gratitude and be in belonging with the land. Thank the moon for her light and the sun for his rise. Find all sorts of big and tiny ways to care for the seas, the trees, the skies.

Be an earth angel for the world. Stay open, pray often, love hard: look between and behind the lines. Stand up for what's right, speak truth in the dark, be vigilant and aware like the deep forest pine—while maintaining awareness that we're here to unite not divide.

Be an earth angel for yourself. Tend your heart, tend your soul, tend you being, tend your mind. Do good things for you without apology, knowing your light deserves to shine. Self-care, radical self-empathy; self-belief, exquisite self-sensitivity. Remember you are an ongoing work of evolving creativity deserving of your care and your time.

Drift. Transform. Transcend. Lift.

Allow your wings to unfold through each act of being love, joy, peace and kind.

WHY I WRITE

I like to find beauty in things other people might dismiss. Find the re-
silience or adaptation in things that may look broken, if you don't
delve beneath the surface to the core of inherent worth. I like to see the
resourcefulness and creativity, and better understand somebody's *why*, and
process, and patterns of being.

I like to gaze at the diamond where others see the rough. Notice the
way it shines all the brighter when starlight hits it in the dark. I like to find
the designs, doodles, and demarcations among the craggy lines in stones,
rocks, and earth's wise face, then piece together the greater pattern being
drawn out.

I like to find grace instead of judgment. Make a melody from discordant
notes. Make a poem from a jumble. Patchwork silk from scraps.

*Find the love in the hard to love. Find the peace in the hard to peace. Find
the gorgeous in the mess. I like to try and find these things within myself as
well as others.*

Mostly I like to find the human in all. The achingly, utterly, chaotic—
each of us is trying so hard—human. Which makes us seek to do life the
best we know how with what we have, as our journeys change, rearrange,
and grow.

I like to find the soul-light beneath, where everything is transmuted by
love's alchemical glow, each of us a work of art creating as we go.

SUPERNOVA

You cannot be afraid of being "too big, too loud, too different" —too "something"—when you need to be that very something to express, actualize, then integrate an aspect of self.

You are not too much, the critics are too little—remember that.

You cannot shine by hiding your light or fear what will happen if you shine too bright. Mold-breakers and game-changers and love-agitators are usually the ones creating lives wrapped in sparkling holiday lights year-round. They keep their own timetables and push past the lines others have drawn to seek authenticity, truth, and expansion.

Mostly you cannot NOT be yourself because some-body else, or some-other else, or some-thing else doesn't get it and wants you to be different. The world needs you—*we need you*—to be your truest self.

You can always be sensitive to other's points of views, and you can always extend others the same grace and right to be in this world that you would like extended to you. But you cannot *not* speak up, lift up, love up, raise up, BE up—and keep yourself suppressed and compressed and repressed, because your growth incites distress.

You have done—*and are doing*—your work to be BIG. So, don't stay small to try and do the work for others. Let the discomfited do their own emotional work to grapple with their own discomfort, and wish them peace and wellness on their journey.

But as for you? Embrace your growth, embrace your soul. Shed and reinvent and agitate with grace. Be bold and be lit. And please be all the "too's" you need to be to keep growing into your gorgeous self.

And shine you fucking Supernova. Shine.

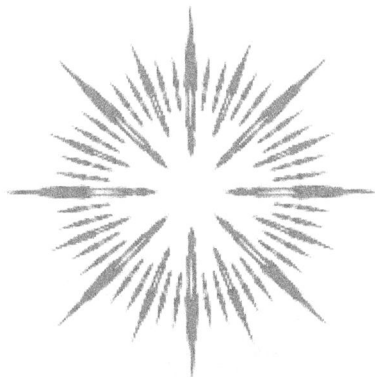

My Dear One, I Believe in You

We are the only ones who can know who we are on the inside. We are the only ones who can learn to embody our truth and walk a path where our internal world is in alignment with our external world.

Being yourself in this world is the most beautiful and the most difficult. It requires so much personal integrity in doing your work and trying to create a life and way of being coherent with your highest truth.

It's a process. One we are all unfolding into. Perfection is unobtainable, and from my perspective undesirable, *because how else will you learn and grow and get bigger?* Progress is marked through the simple act of continuing to show up as best we know how, root out our honest, and deal with what comes up. Then let life support and create with us in becoming wiser, more authentic, more loving beings.

Be brave. Keep showing up for you. Know that many will not get it—and that's totally okay as it's not their path. But the right ones will show up and walk beside you and lend encouragement on the way.

Always remember to keep working on being your own biggest encourager as there is nothing more powerful than saying out loud to yourself:

My dear one, I believe in you.

Your Heart Magic

Follow your heart magic into worlds unknown. Learn your sacred language of soul. Skip to the rhythm of your spirit's drumbeat. Taste the kind nectar of this world's bittersweet.

With your joyful abandon and crystalline wings, become so authentically, beautifully BIG—you have no place to go but up, up, up into sky's rainbow seam. *And there in the cusp of divinity's reach, you'll find the soft grace to set yourself free.*

POSTSCRIPT

The following pieces were originally published in the following publications & places:

Chasing Fairies and *Empress* are in *GODDESS: When She Rules: Expressions by Contemporary Women*, 2017. *The Reluctant Shaman* is in *Hidden Lights: A Collection of Truths Not Often Told*, 2017. *The Sound of Silence* is in *Transformations of The Sun*, 2018.

A few of the pieces in this book were originally published in the curriculum from my online courses. *Into the Woods* and *Intuition's Speak* are from *Cultivating Your Intuition*. *Grief's Doorway* and *Grace Rebels* are from *The Alchemy of Grief*. *Care for the Sensitive Soul* and *Words for Empaths* are from *The Heart of Empathy*.

In *Sundays Are for Silence* the line "boundaries are conventions we're meant to transcend" is inspired by the line "all boundaries are conventions, waiting to be transcended" from the book *Cloud Atlas* by David Mitchell, 2004.

Thank you to Alice from Golden Dragonfly Press for saying yes to this project and making *things of that nature* into a beautiful reality! Carolyn and Laura—my cover reviewers—your words are very much appreciated, your friendship very much cherished.

And to E—thanks for marrying a writer with a mystic heart and moving to an island with me. Here's to many more years on the journey and oceans of feelings and love.

To all others, I will leave you with these words: *Be kind to your soul, mother your whole, nourish your full: and your soul will be kind to the full of you.*

Be well and be love,

Dr. Beth Anne KW

21

Connect with Dr. BethAnne K.W.

Website:	bethannekw.com
IG:	@dr.bethannekw
FB:	Dr. BethAnne KW

For intuitive guidance and updates on my books, courses and speaking events, sign up for my monthly letter!

IntuitiveYOU@bethannekw.com

☞ ALSO BY DR. BETHANNE K.W.

GRIEF & LOSS

LAMENTATIONS OF THE SEA:
111 Passages on Grief, Love, Loss, and Letting Go
Winner of the 2017 Silver Nautilus Award for Grief and Loss

TRANSFORMATIONS OF THE SUN:
122 passages on finding new life after loss

POETRY & PROSE

HELIOTROPE NIGHTS:
Starlight for the Mind and Soul

FREEBIRD FRIDAYS:
A Love Story

CRANBERRY DUSK:
A Journey Of Becoming

HIDDEN LIGHTS ANTHOLOGY:
A Collection of TRUTHS Not Often Told

CHILDREN'S BOOKS

TALLULAH TALKS TO NATURE:
A Tallulah Adventure

FINIS.

www.ingramcontent.com/pod-product-compliance
Lightning Source LLC
Chambersburg PA
CBHW051420090426
42737CB00014B/2758